MIRACLES OF HEALING
IN THE GOSPEL OF MARK

MIRACLES OF HEALING IN THE GOSPEL OF MARK

16 Studies for Individual or Small Group

John I. Penn Sr.

WESTBOW
PRESS®
A DIVISION OF THOMAS NELSON
& ZONDERVAN

WestBow Press books may be ordered through booksellers or by contacting:

WestBow Press
A Division of Thomas Nelson & Zondervan
1663 Liberty Drive
Bloomington, IN 47403
www.westbowpress.com
844-714-3454

ISBN: 978-1-6642-5081-9 (sc)
ISBN: 978-1-6642-5080-2 (e)

Print information available on the last page.

WestBow Press rev. date: 11/24/2021

This book is dedicated to my mother, Josephine Allen. Penn and my wife and best friend, Gloria.

CONTENTS

FOREWORD

§

Y ou hold in your hand a soul-searching, mind-provoking, heart-inspiring, easy-to-read study of the healing miracles in the Gospel of Mark. A traditional approach to Bible reading, this is not. Rather, the author's format of these sixteen healing moments is easy to follow, creatively constructed, and has the potential of motivating the reader to be more alert and sensitive to Christ's miracle-working presence today.

John Penn will expand your understanding of the word and the reality of "miracles." Try not to skip any of his suggested step-by-step design. Simply carve out some quiet, solitude time and do not hurry through this book. Approach each study with a high degree of anticipation, an open spirit, and a willingness to allow the Holy Spirit to communicate with your entire being.

I am gratefully inspired by the author's research, insights, and faithfulness to the Gospel of Jesus Christ.

James K. Wagner, Author
Prayer and Healing books: *Blessed to Be a Blessing, The Spiritual Heart of Your Health;* Former Director of the Disciplined Order of Christ and Upper Room Ministry Staff

AN INTRODUCTION TO
THE GOSPEL OF MARK

§

THE SYNOPTIC GOSPEL

Mark is one of four Gospels: Matthew, Mark, Luke, and John. Although Matthew's gospel is listed first, most scholars now agree that Mark's gospel was the earliest of the four gospels.

The first three gospels are referred to as the synoptic gospels. The word *synoptic* comes from two Greek words which mean *to see together*. [1] When we place their common texts side by side, it becomes apparent that they share similar material, which mirrors each other. In many cases, they are written word for word. There may be a slight variation in some of the words or a minor addition of words. Observing these striking similarities, we can only assume that the three writers got their material in one of two ways: Either the three writers obtained their content from a familiar source, or two of the three writers used a third primary source. This synoptic debate is far from being over. [2]

WHO IS MARK?

Everyone who is about to stand trial in a court of law would want to have on their team the best possible witnesses to support their case. Someone raised a serious question every Christian should be able to answer in the affirmative: *"If you were being tried in a court of law as a Christian, would there be enough evidence to convict you?"* For Christ's sake, we certainly hope that every believer would be found guilty as charged.

Although Mark was not a direct eyewitness of the events of Jesus' life and work, his information is both creditable and trustworthy. Mark obtained his information from a most reliable source—as they say, *"Straight from the horse's mouth"*—the apostle Peter. Peter was one of the original twelve disciples and one of the three disciples invited into Jesus' inner circle.

As one of the first four disciples called by Jesus, Peter was a personal eyewitness of everything Jesus said and did. Peter was with Jesus at the beginning and the end of his earthly mission and ministry, including his death, resurrection, and ascension. He played a significant role in spreading the gospel of Jesus Christ to Roman Jewish Christians, who had scattered about as they faced a variety of trials and tribulations for their faith in Jesus Christ. Scholars agree that Peter played a significant role in preserving Jesus' kingdom work as the Son of God. He is considered one of the greatest of Jesus' twelve apostles.

In the New Testament, we find bits and pieces about Mark, who was best known as John Mark. He was the son of Mary, a woman of some means, who lived in Jerusalem. Mary's home served as the headquarters of the first church in Jerusalem (Acts 12:12). Mark's home was also where Jesus shared the Passover meal with his disciples. Mark grew up in this church house, experiencing the movement and power of God right there in the place he called home. Although Mark was not one of the original disciples, he knew Jesus, many of his disciples, and other church leaders. We know that Peter took a personal interest in Mark and probably served as a mentor.

Mark's home was the meeting place where church members gathered to plan the work of the church, to pray, and to meet when the church faced a crisis.[3] When Peter was in prison, the Christ followers gathered there to pray for his safety and release. And it was Mark's home where Peter went when the angel of the Lord released him from prison (Acts 12:12-19 NRSV).

Barnabas, John Mark's uncle, was aware of his spiritual foundation, his love for the Lord and the early church. Knowing this about Mark, Barnabas was influenced to introduce him to Paul and invite him on their first evangelistic missionary journey. Later, when the team set sail from Paphos and came to Per' ga in Pamphylia, John Mark abruptly left Paul and Barnabas and returned home. Paul and Barnabas went on from Per 'ga and came to Antioch in Pisidia (Acts 13:13-14 NRSV).

By leaving the missionary journey, John Mark caused bad blood between himself and Paul. And eventually, it strained the relationship between, Paul, and Barnabas. On their second missionary journey, Paul and Barnabas decided to revisit and to strengthen all the churches they had started. Barnabas wanted John Mark to rejoin the evangelistic mission team. Paul did not think it was wise to let John Mark rejoin the missionary team because he had once abandoned the mission. His departure probably created a hardship on the rest of the team. Sharply divided, Barnabas took John Mark with him, and Paul chose Silas to travel to Syria and Cilicia (Acts 15:36- 40). This sharp disagreement between Barnabas and Paul prevented them from ever working together again.[4] However, many years later, the relationship between John Mark and Paul was healed, and they were reconciled. As they established a new relationship, Paul acknowledged how valuable John Mark had become to his ministry (2 Tim. 4:11b; Col. 4:10 NRSV).

MARK'S EPIPHANY ON THE MISSION FIELD

John Mark's sudden departure from the mission field created doubt and mistrust in Paul's mind and heart. Some scholars suggest that Mark was a mommy's boy and became homesick. Others said he was too young and inexperienced for such a dangerous mission.[5]

Could it be that Paul misjudged the sincerity and commitment of John Mark to the kingdom work of God?

It is conceivable John Mark's motives for leaving the missionary field had a deeper spiritual reason than the simplistic reasoning Paul and some scholars would have us believe. It seems reasonable that while Mark was out on the mission field, he had an *epiphany.* Having experienced ministry up close and personal, Mark discovered his passion for servant ministry. During that time, Mark was able to hear God's still small voice. His eyes and mind were opened to his call to ministry. This time, the voice of God had become sharper, clearer, and more compelling. The call of God was now undeniable and urgent.

This time, Mark knew he had to respond to the Lord. This evangelistic mission field had inspired and captured Mark's full attention and spiritual imagination. He could now perceive his place and role as a servant in God's kingdom work. Mark went home a changed and more confident man. He went home and reconnected with his friend and mentor, Peter. Peter's fondness for Mark was no secret. Their strong relationship was mutual. Peter affirmed his closeness to Mark, referring to him as *"my son"* (1 Peter 5:13 NRSV).

Mark's return home was a Godsend. He would meet an essential need in Peter's life. Peter recognized Mark's unique skills as a scribe and his knowledge of the Old Testament. Peter's leadership role and demanding schedule had prevented him from writing down his remembrance of Jesus' life, mission, and ministry. Peter used Mark as his scribe to write down and preserve those foundational truths contained in the gospel of Jesus Christ for future generations.

Mark now realized that the Holy Spirit had been leading and guiding his thoughts and actions in leaving the missionary field. God's divine call on his life was now taking shape and making sense. Mark recognized the significance of writing his gospel of Jesus Christ for future generations. For him, nothing was as important as telling others about Jesus, the Son of God—the Messiah of the Jewish people and the world.

Embracing his call as a servant with Peter was a game changer for them both. Understanding our call to servant ministry has eternal consequences in advancing the kingdom of God. Because of his obedience, saying yes to God's call on his life would make Mark's name a household word.

THE DATE AND PLACE OF MARK'S GOSPEL

Over a period of years while in Rome, Mark compiled the story of Jesus' life he had received from the apostle Peter. He wrote his gospel for the Roman people, both Jews and Gentiles. He wrote it so that the common people could relate to it and come to know Jesus as the Son of God— the Messiah. They would learn that Jesus had come to save the Jewish people from their sins, restoring their covenant relationship with the God of their fathers. Mark's gospel was written just shortly after Peter's death around A.D. 65. Most scholars place the writing of Mark's gospel between A.D. 55 and A.D. 70.[6]

THE DISTINCTIVENESS OF MARK'S GOSPEL

Mark wanted his readers to recognize the two natures of Jesus, both human, and divine. He revealed Jesus' divine nature in the opening of his gospel with this statement: *"The beginning of the good news of Jesus Christ, the Son of God" (Mark 1:1 NRSV)*. Mark presented three witnesses to validate who Jesus is. The first witness, John the Baptist (vv.7-8), was a credible witness from the Old Testament prophetic voice of Isaiah: *"See, I am sending my messenger ahead of you, who will prepare your way; the voice of one crying out in the wilderness 'Prepare the way of the Lord, make his paths strait'" (Mark 1:2-3 NRSV; Isa. 40:3)*.

John and Jesus were the only ones who witnessed the Spirit descending on him like a dove from heaven and heard the voice of God proclaiming to Jesus, *"And the Spirit descending like a dove on him. And a voice came from heaven; You are my Son, the Beloved; with you, I am well pleased"* (Mark 1:10-11 NRSV).

The second witness is the voice and action of God. John baptized Jesus in the Jordan, and when he came up out of the water, *"he saw the heavens were torn apart" (Mark 1:10 NRSV)* and God referring to Jesus as his *Son,* the most beloved title of the Christian community.

The third witness of Jesus is the Holy Spirit who sent him into the desert for forty days to be tempted by Satan (v. 12). Jesus came to usher in the kingdom of God. He came to bring God's salvation, first, to the Jewish people and, through them, to bring salvation to the nations of the world.[7]

Mark distinguished Jesus from all the other human servants of God. He did so by emphasizing Jesus' unique relationship with God, whom he called Father. Jesus' words and deeds, including his miracles, power, and authority, all point to his unique relationship with his Father. Mark also pointed out that the people recognized Jesus did not teach like the other Jewish religious leaders. His teachings amazed the people. They even questioned who gave him such wisdom. The people marveled at the power and authority of his words and deeds (Mark 1:22, 27 NRSV). Mark also wanted his readers to see the human side of Jesus.

Jesus was the carpenter's son from Nazareth (Mark 6:1). Mark was the only gospel writer who showed the emotional side of Jesus. After being in the wilderness for forty days, he was hungry. Jesus displayed love and compassion for those who were suffering, like sheep without a shepherd (Mark 6:34).[8] He had a human family, including brothers, sisters, and a mother (Mark 3:30-31).

One of Mark's favorite words used in the KJV was *straightway.* It occurred in his gospel about forty times. Mark showed Jesus on the move, doing many activities as if each word and deed were an urgent matter. Jesus was focused on fulfilling his divine mission. His mission was to defeat the work of Satan, to proclaim the good news of salvation to the Jewish people, and through them, to spread salvation to all nations. His mission was the restoration of God's good creation. Mark said that Jesus did not come for the strong who did not need a physician, but for those who were sick and needed a doctor (Mark 2:17).

Mark's gospel can be easily distinguished from the other three gospels. There is the absence of a birth story or genealogy. Mark used the fewest number of words or smaller amount of material, containing the life, teachings, and deeds of Jesus. Mark's gospel was written for the Greek-speaking people in Rome who were unfamiliar with the Semitic languages of Palestine (Aramaic and Hebrew). Where Mark did use words from Hebrew languages (Aramaic or Hebrew), he always interpreted them for his readers.[6] Some examples are the Aramaic words "*Talitha cumi,*" which means "Little girl, get up" (5:41), or "*Abba,*" for "Father" (Mark 14:36 NRSV), or " *'löi, E'löi, lema'sabach'thani,*" meaning "My God, my God, why have you forsaken me?" (Mark 15:34 NRSV).

The unique two-step process of healing a blind man is found only in Mark (see 8:22-26). After laying his hands on the man's eyes, he received only partial healing. Jesus then laid his hand on him a second time, and the man's vision was completely restored.

THE CONFUSION ABOUT THE MISSING ENDING OF MARK

The two endings of Mark's gospel in Chapter 16—the shorter ending at verse 8 with the longer ending continuing from verses 9 to 20—have brought about much debate. The short ending of Mark's gospel has strong support. There are several concerns with trying to reconcile the transition between Mark16:9-20, the more extended version, with 16:1-8, the shorter version. First, the internal evidence strongly indicates that verses 9-20 seem odd and out of place with the earlier material. Second, most older sources show that verses 9-20 are absent in the older most reliable Greek manuscripts. Third, the fourth-century Christian historian, Eusebius, also confirm this finding, noting that the longer ending was missing from "most all MSS" Greek resources at his disposal. Fourth, other early Christian writers, including Clement of Alexandria, Origen, Cyprian, and Cyril of Jerusalem do not know this more extended ending. Fifth, the more prolonged text is absent in two of the earliest parchment codices, Vaticanus (B) and Sinaiticus (א).[7]

Sixth, although Mary Magdalene has been mentioned three times in the earlier verses, she now appears in verse 9, as if for the first time, casting doubt on Mark's authorship. Finally, the writer introduces several Greek words in verses 9-20 that are not found anywhere else in Mark's Gospel. Some scholars suggest that Mark did not have an opportunity to get the ending to the gospel because something had happened to Peter, preventing him from sharing the last details of the gospel. Perhaps Peter had been arrested and executed.[8]

Although feasible, many scholars have rejected this argument. They agree the original ending of Mark did not need further material because the resurrection of Jesus had taken place with sufficient evidence: the angel who said Jesus had risen witnessed to it, the empty tomb witnessed to it, and the three women who heard and believed the angel's testimony. They left the tomb with both terror and amazement. They accepted the message given to them by the angels and said nothing to anyone because they were afraid (Mark 16:8).

Mark ended his gospel at verse eight because he believed Jesus Christ, the Son of God, had triumphed over death and there was nothing else to be said. Jesus' earthly ministry is finished. Mark began his gospel by announcing that Jesus is the Son of God. He ended his gospel—at 16:8—by showing that Jesus had finished his redemptive work by dying on the cross. God raised him from the dead on the third day, as he had said he would. His resurrection had been predicted in accordance with the Scriptures. (See Mark 10:45; 1 Cor. 15:3.) Mark realized that the resurrection was a matter of faith alone. The apostle Paul comes to this same conclusion that belief in the resurrection is a matter of faith. He states:

> *"Now if Christ is proclaimed as raised from the dead, how can some of you say there is no resurrection of the dead? If there is no resurrection of the dead, then Christ has not been raised; and if Christ has not been raised, then our proclamation has been in vain, and your faith has been in vain. We are even found to be misrepresenting God because we testified of God that he raised Christ—whom he did not raise if it is true that the dead are not raised. For if the dead are not raised, then Christ has not been raised. If Christ has not been raised, your faith is futile, and you are still in your sins" (1 Cor. 15:12-17 NRSV).*

If you believe in the miracles of Jesus, then it is reasonable to accept him as the Son of God. One must accept by faith that the resurrection happened, and because of the resurrection, God will also raise us from the dead. The resurrection is a faith issue. Because of his resolve, Jesus conferred his power and authority to his apostles and sent the Holy Spirit to empower them to continue his kingdom work. The resurrected Christ is incarnated in his church—the priesthood of all believers. Christ Jesus continues his kingdom work through his body, the church, and through the power of the Holy Spirit. Christ promised to be with the church to the end of the age (Matt. 28:18-20).

Finally, through the power of the Holy Spirit, the church reveals the real presence of Jesus Christ. The church, the body of Christ, functions as Christ's hands, feet, and voice. Jesus has empowered the church to continue his threefold ministry of teaching, preaching, and healing until he returns (Mark 3:16-19; 6:7-11; Matt. 10:1; 9-14; Luke 9:1, 3-5; 10:1-9, 17-20). Through the church, Jesus Christ still calls people to repent and receive the good news of the kingdom, the gospel of salvation, first to the Jews, and through the Jews, to spread God's salvation to all the nations.

INTRODUCTION

❧

Before deciding to write this book, *Miracles of Healing in the Gospel of Mark*, I had written three different partial drafts of a book on healing. I had known for some time that I would eventually write a book on healing but finding the right approach and direction for the book was unclear. My desire to write a book on healing and wholeness had been incubating within my heart, mind, and spirit for several years. This period gave me pause to step back and allow the incubation process to continue.

I used this time to pray, to reflect, and to be aware of the leading and direction of the Holy Spirit. The guidance of the Holy Spirit proved to be invaluable and assured me of God's direction. My attention was drawn to the healing stories recorded in the gospel of Mark. Gradually, I began to sense this was the direction I should take. What a joyful revelation! As I started to read the healing miracles as told by Mark, I saw things I had never seen before. These discoveries and insights captured my heart and mind. As I gave my full attention to reading, studying, and researching the healing miracles in Mark's gospel, under the guidance and inspiration of the Holy Spirit, a fresh and new perspective began to emerge. I could sense a paradigm shift taking place in my thinking.

Through the years, I have read over seventy-five books on healing—and some I read several times. In addition to this, I have written several books and booklets on healing. For twenty-five years, God has given me opportunities to teach about healing in over sixty churches, across denominational lines, throughout the United States and in many places around the world, including Africa, Chili, Cuba, Brazil, Mexico, Scotland, Ireland, and Panama.

In addition to teaching on healing in many churches, I have also designed and taught courses on healing and wholeness at two seminaries, Wesley Theological Seminary in Washington, D.C. and Asbury Theological Seminary in Wilmore, KY. Although I have retired and am no longer pastoring a church, I am still teaching and writing articles and books on healing. I consider it a blessing to have this opportunity to write this book on healing because healing is an essential and vital ministry of the church of Christ.

Early on in my study, it became evident that Mark was not simply recounting the healing incidents that Jesus had performed. Mark looked at the healing miracles of Jesus through the lens of God's perspective. What was significant to Mark and what captured my spiritual imagination was his interpretation of the healing miracles. He made it clear to the readers that Jesus clearly understood the redemptive implications of his mission as the Jewish healer-redeemer. Jesus fully embraced his Messianic mission to bring salvation to the Hebrew people. He would become the perfect sacrificial lamb of God to bring about the restoration of fallen humanity. In and through him, God's good creation would be restored.

Through Jesus' sacrificial death, God would create a new covenant of grace, which could be acceptable to both Jews and Gentiles. The healing miracles demonstrated the defeat of sin, sickness, death, and the evil influence of Satan's demonic forces. Jesus did this by not only removing our sins but also taking the consequences of our sins upon himself, nailing them to the cross. All of Jesus' healing miracles were interpreted similarly. I found Mark's gospel both inspiring and informative, allowing me to see the heart, love, compassion, and mind of God for His creation.

It is noteworthy that Mark begins his account of Jesus' public kingdom work with the healing of a man possessed by an unclean spirit. It is also significant that this healing occurred in the synagogue on the sabbath. Healing by exorcism was a central part of the ministry of Jesus, according to Mark's gospel. Healing by exorcism was calculated and essential to God's kingdom in several ways.

First, exorcism was central to the kingdom work of God. Healing defined Jesus' divine mission as the Messiah of God. Second, healing was a sign that the kingdom of God had broken into human history. Third, the exorcisms showed the continuous conflict between the kingdom of God and the kingdom of Satan. Fourth, Mark interpreted healing and salvation as being inseparable. Biblically and theologically, they represent the two sides of the same coin. Fifth, the healing miracles demonstrated that Satan's evil kingdom is no match for the kingdom of God. Sixth, Mark emphasized that healing would not only be central to the kingdom work of Jesus, but also for the church, the body of Christ. And seventh, the gospel of Mark demonstrated that Jesus healed the whole person. It is essential to understand that Jesus treated exorcism as more of a cure than a punishment.[1]

Most importantly, exorcism points us to an age-old conflict between God and Satan that goes back to the creation story and the fall of humanity. When the serpent questioned God's sovereignty and tempted Eve to disobey God's warning, which she did, sin was introduced into God's good creation. Sin has caused all of creation to fall from the perfect order in which God had created it. God sent Jesus, the seed of the woman, to restore God's ultimate intent for creation.

Therefore Jesus "first public act" of exorcism (healing) looked back to the fall of humanity and looked forward to the cross, when God's perfect order of creation would be restored, which looks toward a glorious future. It is important to remember that initially, creation was void of sin, sickness, and death. In the new divine order of creation, all sin, sickness, and death will be prohibited.

The apostle Paul foresaw a future where all human brokenness, including creation would be restored to a magnificent future:

> *For the creation waits with eager longing for the revealing of the children of God; for the creation was subjected to futility, not of its own will but by the will of the one who subjected it, in hope that the creation itself will be set free from its bondage to decay and will obtain the freedom of the glory of the children of God. [22] We know that the whole creation has been groaning in labor pains until now; and not only the creation, but we ourselves, who have the first fruits of the Spirit, groan inwardly while we wait for adoption, the redemption of our bodies. For in hope we were saved.* (Rom. 8:19-24 NRSV.)

Without understanding this biblical interpretation, healing will always have a secondary role in the life, mission, and ministry of the church, which is contrary to the gospel of Jesus Christ. Jesus gave healing a prominent place and role in the kingdom work of God.

Mark's gospel may be the simplest written and shortest in content or resources of information of the synoptic gospels, yet it is by no means the least important. Although Mark's gospel is placed second, behind the gospel of Matthew, scholars agree that Mark's gospel is the earliest of the surviving gospels. It faithfully preserved the most essential facts concerning the life, mission, death, and resurrection of Jesus' earthly mission and ministry.

Healing Moment One, "The Healing Power of Jesus' Words" makes it clear that Satan and his demonic forces are no match for the power and authority of Jesus. Mark answered the question, "Why do bad things happen to good people." In fact, Jesus named Satan as the veiled evil behind the bad things. Mark's gospel made it clear that the casting out of demons demonstrates that the kingdom of God has broken into human history.

Healing Moment Two, "God's Amazing Grace" proclaims that God provided Jesus with divine power and authority to cast out demons and to heal people with a variety of diseases, manifesting the presence of God at work in the person of Jesus Christ. Jesus not only spoke for God but also acted for God. Jesus was given by God the power and authority to heal all who are oppressed by the devil (Acts 10:38). He conferred his authority to his followers to be witnesses to his resurrected presence in the world.

Healing Moment Three, "Jesus Identifies with Human Brokenness" reminds us that healing is in the atonement. According to the prophet Isaiah, Jesus took our sins and sickness in his own body, as the perfect lamb of God, nailing them to the cross. This healing story reminds us that by touching the leper, Jesus identified with the leper's humanity and brokenness. The healing miracles tell us of God's providential care toward humankind.

Healing Moment Four, "The Healing Power of Forgiveness" emphasizes the importance of forgiveness. Jesus' healing of the paralytic man witnesses to the fact that God looks beyond our faults and sees our need for healing, wholeness, and salvation. Restoring our relationship with God and to each other is one of the ways people may experience healing, personally and corporately.

Healing Moment Five, "Healing Is Always Lawful" reveals that it is always right to do good. Jesus told the Pharisees that doing good always supersedes human traditions. He admonished the religious leaders for their strict interpretation of the sabbath law. He reminded them that the sabbath was made for man and not the other way around.

Healing Moment Six, "Jesus Empowers His Disciples to Heal" reminds us that Jesus fully believed God would empower his followers to do the work of the kingdom, just as God had empowered Jesus.

Jesus conferred his authority upon the disciples to continue his kingdom work in the church and the world.

Healing Moment Seven, "Jesus' Power Knows No Bounds" teaches that God is not a respecter of persons. God loves people unconditionally and desires their highest good. Jesus died on the cross for the sins of the whole world. God sent Jesus into the world so that all people would experience wholeness in every dimension of life and live with God for eternity.

Healing Moment Eight, "A Faith That Would Not Be Denied" points out that God rewards faith. God is not indifferent to the needs of humanity. There is nothing too small or too hard for Jesus to handle. We can bring our insufficiencies to the all-sufficient Christ. The healing stories remind us that nothing is too hard or impossible with God. Jesus not only healed everyone who was sick but often involved those he healed in their healing process. Jesus always looked for an opportunity to connect God's power with human needs.

Healing Moment Nine, "Jesus' Supreme Power over Death" highlights the raising of Jarius's daughter from the dead and gives assurance that for those who are in Christ, not even death can separate them from the love of God that is in Christ Jesus. As the parents faced the death of their daughter, Jesus spoke these comforting and powerful words: *"Do not fear, only believe" (Mk. 5:36)*

Healing Moment Ten, "Jesus' Disciples as God's Healers" affirms that the Christian life is a shared life in Christ. Jesus fully anticipated that the Church would continue his kingdom work, both in the church and the world. He sent the gift of the Holy Spirit for that very purpose. Jesus gave the church a mandate to go into the world and make disciples of all nations, baptizing them in the name of the Father, Son, and the Holy Spirit. Then he said, "I am with you always, even to the end of the age" (Matt. 28:20 NRSV).

Healing Moment Eleven, "Healing Faith, Not Magic" makes the case that an unspiritual person cannot comprehend or accept spiritual matters. Even believers need the help or aid of the Holy Spirit to receive the things of God. Mark makes it clear that God responds to faith and not magic. Magic is manipulation that may give the appearance of faith and leads to all kinds of confusion and dependence on self and not on God. God heals us because He loves us. God's love cannot be manipulated or earned. Healing is a means of grace. God heals because He loves humanity unconditionally. God desires and seeks our highest good.

Healing Moment Twelve, "Persistent Healing Faith" challenges us to have persistent and expectant faith. God rewards lively, expectant faith. The New Testament discourages unbelief or faithlessness. In the epistle of James, we are told that a person without faith will not receive anything from God. In the book of Hebrews, we read that without faith it is impossible to please God. The Syrophoenician woman displayed persistent faith. Jesus was so impressed with her strong, persistent faith that he healed her daughter without praying, touching, or being in the presence of her daughter. Mark's gospel emphasizes over and over that God rewards faith and does not respond to unbelief or faithlessness.

Healing Moment Thirteen, "God's Healing Grace Includes Everyone" makes it clear that the gospel of Jesus Christ is inclusive. God's love is universal. God loves humanity unconditionally. Jesus proved this by dying on a cross for the sins of the whole world. Jesus healed all who turned to him to be healed, both Jews and Gentiles alike. Although he was the Jewish Messiah, he was also the savior of the world. His mission was first to the Jews and through the Jews to spread the gospel of salvation to the entire world. Salvation is ultimate healing. The fact that Gentiles are being healed is evident that Jesus Christ is the savior of the world.

Healing Moment Fourteen, "A Miracle That Required Two Attempts" demonstrates the power of unbelief. Mark told us that Jesus could only heal a few folks in Bethsaida because of the lack of faith. Some may question why he did not heal there, but by examining themselves, they may conclude that their lifestyles are not pleasing to Jesus Christ. Seeking healing should suggest that people don't just want to be partially healed, but to become a whole person.

Healing Moment Fifteen, "Prayer, Not Human Power, Overcomes Demons" speaks volumes that Jesus is our present help in the time of trouble. Jesus came to set the captives free. He has defeated all our enemies and has empowered us to set others free. Mark makes it clear that those who have put their faith and trust in God through Christ know they have the same power and authority to resist and defeat Satan's evil forces. We are more than conquerors through Christ Jesus who strengthens us. We can face the future with confidence and peace.

The final Healing Moment is "Your Faith Has Made You Well." Because of the strong faith of blind Bartimaeus, Jesus told him, "Go, your faith has made you well." Bartimaeus teaches us that we are not to listen to the naysayers but to put our faith in the healing Christ, the Great Physician. He also teaches that we are not to allow our fears to cause us to throw in the towel when we face challenges and uncertainty. Bartimaeus challenges us to turn to a loving God who sacrificed His Son to reveal his love and care on behalf of humanity. God caused His Son to suffer pain and separation from his Father and to die for sinners. This proves God's love and care for even the least of us.

I hope that you read this book with an open heart and mind. Some of the concepts in this book might be new to you, but I can assure you that what is contained here is biblical and will challenge your faith to receive your healing. The writing of this book has been a labor of love.

What you put into this study is what you will get out of it. This book was designed to help you to see healing from God's perspective. My goal for this book is to help you to see the big picture of understanding why God made healing a central part of Jesus' kingdom work. The presupposition of this book is twofold. One, healing is rooted in God's amazing and unconditional love for humanity. Two, healing is in the atonement. God sent the world a healing Messiah. God's response to sin was salvation. Salvation is ultimate healing.

I hope you will use what you have learned to walk in wholeness in every dimension of life: spirit, body, mind (including emotions), and relationships. It is also my hope that you will allow God to use you as an instrument to bring healing to others as a sign of the gospel of Christ—the gospel of salvation. Remember, you don't have to know everything about healing, to be an instrument of God's healing grace. All you need to do is to love people, believe in the presence of a loving and caring God, and healing happens.

THE HEALING POWER OF JESUS' WORDS

§

CONTEMPLATION

Throughout human history, people have asked the question, "Why do bad things happen to good people?" It seems that evil always triumphs over good. In the book of Job, this question is thoroughly considered and answered.

Mark's gospel challenged the wisdom of this statement. In fact, Mark reveals that Jesus emphatically answered this question in healing the man oppressed by an unclean spirit. Jesus named Satan as the veiled evil behind the bad things. He did not debate the issue or ring his hands over it. He confronted Satan and took the first step toward exposing and overthrowing his evil kingdom with the power and authority of God. This exorcism follows up Jesus' defeat of Satan in the wilderness, demonstrating that Satan is no match against the power of God. The casting out of the demons amazed the people. The fact that he commanded even unclean spirits and they obeyed him caused the people who witnessed the exorcism to question who Jesus was and where his authority came from.[1]

BACKGROUND

Mark's gospel reveals that the synagogue is not just a place to pray, to read Scripture, and to hear an explanation of it. Jesus demonstrated that the Synagogue is also a place to experience the presence and healing power of God. The man oppressed by an unclean spirit discovered that when the scriptures are rightly interpreted, and one's mind and heart are fertile ground for the word of God to be planted and watered, miracles are possible, and lives are transformed. This man was at the right place at the right time. Mark reminds us that worship should always be a time to experience the presence and power of God.

A HEALING MOMENT

Read Mark 1:21-28 from the NRSV or the NKJV.

NRSV

[21] They went to Capernaum; and when the sabbath came, he entered the synagogue and taught. [22] They were astounded at his teaching, for he taught them as one having authority, and not as the scribes. [23] Just then there was in their synagogue a man with an unclean spirit, [24] and he cried out, "What have you to do with us, Jesus of Nazareth? Have you come to destroy us? I know who you are, the Holy One of God." [25] But Jesus rebuked him, saying, "Be silent, and come out of him!" [26] And the unclean spirit, convulsing him and crying with a loud voice, came out of him. [27] They were all amazed, and they kept on asking one another, "What is this? A new teaching—with authority! He commands even the unclean spirits, and they obey him." [28] At once his fame began to spread throughout the surrounding region of Galilee.

NKJV

[21] Then they went into Capernaum, and immediately on the sabbath He entered the synagogue and taught. [22] And they were astonished at His teaching, for He taught them as one having authority, and

not as the scribes.[23] *Now there was a man in their synagogue with an unclean spirit. And he cried out,* [24] *saying, "Let us alone! What have we to do with You, Jesus of Nazareth? Did You come to destroy us? I know who You are—the Holy One of God!"* [25] *But Jesus rebuked him, saying, "Be quiet, and come out of him!"* [26] *And when the unclean spirit had convulsed him and cried out with a loud voice, he came out of him.* [27] *Then they were all amazed, so that they questioned among themselves, saying, "What is this? What new doctrine is this? For with authority, He commands even the unclean spirits, and they obey Him."* [28] *And immediately His fame spread throughout all the region around Galilee.*

DISCOVERY

1. 1. What about the healing of the man oppressed by an unclean spirit is so significant as Jesus' first action to begin his public mission as the Messiah, the Son of God?

2. When Jesus demonstrated his authority over demons, what did the people who witnessed it learn about him? How is this important for the church?

3. What do demons know about Jesus that surprised you?

4. How is this healing miracle a game changer for the kingdom of Satan and the kingdom of God?

5. What does this miracle reveal about God's attitude concerning sickness and human brokenness? (See Acts 10:38.)

6. Is God's authority over demons available to Christian believers today? (See Mark 3:13-19; Luke 9:1-2; 10:17-20; 1 Cor. 12:9, 10).

7. Who in your church do people turn to when they suspect demon activity in their own life or that of a loved one?

ENCOURAGEMENT

We have learned from the Gospel of Mark that Jesus fully accepted his unique calling as the Son of God. He embraced his messianic mission as liberator, healer, advocate of the poor, and savior of suffering humanity.

What makes Jesus' story so unique is his total dependence on God's power and authority. He understood that he was fighting God's battle against the evils of human pain and suffering, which Satan is behind. He confronted the status quo and challenged evil on every front. Jesus always looked for opportunities to lift up the oppressed, the poor, and the sick. His kingdom work gave people hope, signaling that they were not alone or helpless. God is on the side of the oppressed. This healing miracle reveals a paradigm shift, demonstrating the arrival of God's kingdom and marking the end of Satan's reign on earth.

RESPONSE

8. What role should the church play in the practice of deliverance? (See Matt. 10:1-2; Mark 3:14-15; Luke 9:1-2; 10:8-9, 17-20; Acts 10:38; 1 Cor. 12:9.) As disciples of Jesus Christ, what does it mean to have God's power and authority to set persons free from demonic activities?

9. How has God gifted and equipped the church to continue Jesus' ministry of healing to those oppressed by the devil?

10. Describe what you will take away from this Healing Moment that has given you hope and assurance that Jesus has defeated all our enemies, including demonic oppression.

GOING DEEPER

Perhaps you have read this healing story many times before without considering the significance of why Mark chose exorcism as Jesus' first miracle to begin his ministry. Mark wanted to show the power and authority of Jesus as the Son of God, the Messiah who was to come.[2]

The healing ministry is a natural progression of Jesus confronting and defeating Satan in the wilderness. As Jesus said, healing is a sign that the kingdom of God has come near. Healing is a demonstration of God's kingdom work in the person of Jesus Christ and the dismantling of Satan's kingdom. The coming of the kingdom of God is a paradigm shift in human history.[3]

It is my interpretation of Genesis Chapter 3:1-24 NRSV, that God initiated the course of action against the sins of the serpent (Satan) and Adam and Eve. God decided the woman's seed would bruise the serpent's (Satan) head for deceiving Eve. Jesus is that Seed. Mark made it clear that Jesus was chosen and anointed by God to resolve this conflict between God and Satan.[4] God initiated the resolution of this conflict, and put it into motion on God's terms, to be achieved in God's way, to satisfy God's righteous justice. Mark included several exorcism incidents in his gospel to emphasize the continuous conflict between Jesus and the forces of Satan. Mark also showed that Satan knows his kingdom is coming to an end. As a created angel, he and his fallen angels are under God's control. They cannot do anything unless God allows it. Their purpose on earth is to prevent, distort, or destroy people's relationship with God.[5]

Even a casual observation of our world reveals that something is seriously wrong and disturbing. Hatred and racism; longstanding religious conflicts; the rise of Isis and other radical groups spreading terror and fear; political chaos and financial uncertainty; poverty; sickness; and disease—all point to an evil, often hidden that is rampant and out of control. The writer of Revelation tells us that the devil has turned his wrath against the inhabitants of the earth because he knows that his kingdom is ending (Rev. 12:12, NRSV). Jesus Christ is the only source that can destroy the works of Satan (John 10:10 NRSV).

According to Mark, all healings are signs that God's kingdom rule, or reign, has broken into human history. Mark also emphasized that Jesus imparted his power and authority to his disciples to continue God's kingdom work against Satan and all the manifestations of human oppression and evil.

Finally, Mark showed that Jesus' words and deeds demonstrated the very power and presence of God, working in the affairs of humanity. The healing miracles show that God's good creation is being restored through the kingdom work of Jesus Christ. Jesus not only acts for God, but he also speaks for God. Mark wanted his readers to know that to see Jesus is to see God. Jesus is their way to God. He is their path to salvation. God has come among humankind in the very person of Jesus Christ. He has come to reveal God's unconditional love to humanity.

Having said all of this, it is imperative for this point to be made. Francis MacNutt made an important observation concerning our need for both the healing Christ and Christ as savior. Because of the fallen condition of humanity, we cannot make it on our own. MacNutt pointed out that the gospel is clear concerning this fact. He said, "We need grace, salvation, healing, and deliverance."[6]

It is important to understand that Jesus considered exorcism as more of a cure than a judgment or punishment.[7] Why? Because Jesus understood that in most cases, oppressed people are not regarded as evil in themselves, but are victims of Satan's diabolical scheme. [8]

DEVOTION
Healing God, thank you for sending us a healing Messiah, Jesus Christ, who both heals, sets the captive free, and saves. He has the

power to heal with a single word. Even demons obey his words. Jesus has proven that Your power and authority have no equals. May your will be done and may your Kingdom come on earth as in heaven. In him, we have the Great Physician To turn to for healing, wholeness, and salvation. In Jesus' name, I pray. Amen.

JOURNALING
To prepare for the next study, read Mark 1:29-39 and complete the questions for Healing Moment Two. Please pray for the participants and facilitators. Be prepared to have a lively discussion.

How has God equipped and gifted you to liberate oppressed people?

GOD'S AMAZING HEALING GRACE

§

CONTEMPLATION

Many in my generation are experiencing the health chal-lenges of our aging parents, or our grandparents, if we are fortunate to still have them with us. All of us who have one or both of our parents living should count our blessings and give them all the love and our presence we can. We only get one chance with our elderly parents. It is important not to have any regrets. Give your roses and your presence while you can.

My mother celebrated her ninety-third birthday on July 30th. What a blessing it is for her eight children to have our mother's presence. Mother has been blessed to share in the joys, accom-plishments, marriages, births, and deaths of many generations in her family. We are truly blessed to have Mom in our lives. Both of my wife's parents are with the Lord in heaven.

Mother still has some health problems, yet she has more good days than bad days. We thank God every day for her life and longevity. Mother's health is assisted by the loving support of her eight children, a hired caregiver, lots of pills, and a sharp mind and wit. We are thankful and celebrate each day we have our mother with us. She is a blessing to the family as well as to her neighbors and friends.

In this scripture passage, we are not sure whether Peter's biological parents are still living. However, Peter still has the presence of his mother-in-law, who is living with his family. When Peter and his guests, including Jesus, have left the synagogue and arrived home, Peter learns that his mother-in-law is sick in bed, with a very high fever. After telling Jesus, he goes into minister to her.

BACKGROUND

On the Sabbath, Jesus went to the synagogue in Capernaum as was his custom. Recognized as a gifted and talented teacher, he was given the scroll to read. The Jewish people were amazed at Jesus' authoritative teaching. His teaching made the scriptures relevant and practical to their everyday lives. Jesus' words and deeds manifested the power and authority of God. When Jesus spoke and acted, even demons had to pause and take notice. They were disturbed by his teaching.

Having just witnessed the miracle-working power of Jesus, the people left the synagogue, spreading the news about Jesus' miracles in the surrounding regions of Galilee. Leaving the synagogue, Jesus, James, and John went to the home of Andrew and Peter. Arriving there, Jesus was told that Peter's mother-in-law was in bed with a high fever (Luke 4:38). Jesus wasted no time. He went to her, took her by the hand, and lifted her up. Miraculously, the fever was removed. Cured of a life-threatening illness, Peter's mother-in-law showed her gratitude to Jesus. She prepared a meal for Peter's guests.

That evening after sunset, many sick and demon-possessed people were brought to the house for Jesus to heal. Jesus healed them all, regardless of their physical conditions. He also cast out many demons and did not allow them to speak because they knew him (vv. 32-34). Those people experienced God's healing grace and so can you!

A HEALING MOMENT
Read Mark 1:29-39 from the NRSV or the NKJV.

NRSV

²⁹ As soon as they left the synagogue, they entered the house of Simon and Andrew, with James and John. ³⁰ Now Simon's mother-in-law was in bed with a fever, and they told him about her at once. ³¹ He came and took her by the hand and lifted her up. Then the fever left her, and she began to serve them. ³² That evening, at sunset, they brought to him all who were sick or possessed with demons. ³³ And the whole city was gathered around the door. 3 4 And he cured many who were sick with various diseases and cast out many demons; and he would not permit the demons to speak, because they knew him.³⁵ In the morning, while it was still very dark, he got up and went out to a deserted place, and there he prayed. ³⁶ And Simon and his companions hunted for him. ³⁷ When they found him, they said to him, "Everyone is searching for you." ³⁸ He answered, "Let us go on to the neighboring towns, so that I may proclaim the message there also; for that is what I came out to do." ³⁹ And he went throughout Galilee, proclaiming the message in their synagogues and casting out demons.

NKJV

²⁹Now as soon as they had come out of the synagogue, they entered the house of Simon and Andrew, with James and John. ³⁰ But Simon's wife's mother lay sick with a fever, and they told Him about her at once. ³¹ So He came and took her by the hand and lifted her up, and immediately the fever left her. And she served them. ³² At evening, when the sun had set, they brought to Him all who were sick and those who were demon-possessed. ³³ And the whole city was gathered together at the door. ³⁴ Then He healed many who were sick with various diseases and cast out many demons; and He did not allow the demons to speak, because they knew Him. ³⁵ Now in the morning, having risen a long while before daylight, He went out and departed to a solitary place; and there He prayed. ³⁶ And Simon and those who were with Him searched for Him. ³⁷ When they found Him, they said to Him, "Everyone is looking for You." ³⁸ But He said to them, "Let us go into the next towns, that I may preach there also because for this purpose I have come forth." ³⁹ And He was preaching in their synagogues throughout all Galilee, and casting out demons."

DISCOVERY

1. Read about this healing story in the gospels of Matthew (8:14-17) and Luke (4:38-41). Make notes of their differences and similarities.

2. Mark packed the healing of Peter's mother-in-law with much hidden and interesting information. Use your detective skills to see how much you can uncover.

3. What did Peter's mother-in-law teach us about how to show our thanks and gratitude to God for the many blessings He bestows on us through Jesus?

4. Even the demonic realm recognized who Jesus is and where he had come from. What blinded the eyes and minds of the people Jesus came to redeem from recognizing him as their Messiah, even though they had witnessed the miracles?

5. What would our world look and feel like without God's healing presence and grace?

6. Is there a difference between sickness and demonic possession?

ENCOURAGEMENT

The Greek word *sózó* can be translated into English as healing, health, wholeness, salvation, deliverance, or well-being. God's optimum plan for the well-being of humanity was compromised in the Fall. The Fall not only compromised the relationship between God and human beings, but it also introduced sin, sickness, and death into God's good creation. It is important to understand that sin has eternal consequences, which require a Godkind of solution. Jesus is that solution. It is important to keep in mind that God's wholeness is central to God's good creation. God sent Jesus to restore that goodness which was lost in the Fall. Remember, the name Jesus in Hebrew is *Joshua*, which means salvation. Jesus came not only to save but to heal God's fractured humanity. To save is to heal, and to heal is to save. They are one and the same. Even in the fall of humanity, God's love and care for humanity have always been at the forefront of everything God has done in words and deeds. God hates the sin but loves the sinner. That love is expressed in every covenant God has entered into with his people. Even when God's people break their part of the covenant, God remains faithful. Healing is a constant sign that God keeps His covenant agreements even with sinful and unfaithful humanity. This is an expression of unconditional love.

Jesus' death on a cross is the ultimate expression of God's covenant love. God's covenant love is manifested in the gospel of the kingdom— salvation, God's ultimate response to sin. Therefore, healing is a central part of Christ's mission and ministry as God's Messiah. Therefore, Jesus never refused to heal anyone because he knew that healing was God's will. Healing and salvation represent God's unconditional love, powerfully demonstrated through the cross. Jesus' death on the cross atoned for human sin, including its consequences. Those who have turned to God for forgiveness have had their transgressions removed. They have been declared righteous and will live eternally with God in the resurrection. (See Rom. 5:12-21; 1 Cor. 15.)

Although sin, evil, and death have been prevalent in our fallen state, God destroyed them through the cross, removing the curse all of humanity are born under. The apostle Paul reminded believers that because of the cross, nothing can separate us from God's love, which is in Christ Jesus. Paul put it in this context:

> *Who shall separate us from the love of Christ? Shall tribulation, or distress, or persecution, or famine, or nakedness, or peril, or sword? ... For I am persuaded that neither death nor life, nor angels nor principalities nor powers, nor things present nor things to come, shall be able to separate us from the love of God which is in Christ Jesus our Lord (Rom. 8:35-36, 38 NKJV; also see Isa. 44:22).*

Through the cross, everything that was lost in the Fall has been restored. Sin, sickness, evil, and death are no longer a threat to God's good creation. This is why Jesus has the authority to heal the sick and to cast out demons. Jesus has given this same authority to his disciples to continue his kingdom work against God's enemies and to call people to repent and receive the gospel of salvation. Fallen humanity has been made right with God through the cross and is now partners with Jesus Christ. The Holy Spirit has empowered God's people with *charismata* (gifts) to demonstrate God's authority in the spiritual realm over the evil of this fallen world. God has given the church gifts of healings as a continuous sign of God's restored creation.

RESPONSE

7. Knowing that the sin problem has been atoned for through the cross, what sin in your life prevents you from experiencing God's healing grace?

8. Jesus healed all the people who were brought to him with a word or touch. How has Jesus healed you?

9. Why did the townspeople wait until the sun went down to bring the sick to be healed by Jesus?

10. What role does faith play in the healing process?

11. How are you caring for the physical and spiritual well-being of the elderly in your family, church, and the community?

GOING DEEPER

Jesus clearly understood his mission and accepted its daunting and enormous challenge. He visited many homes during his ministry, yet, as he put it, "the Son of Man has nowhere to lay his head" (Matt. 8:20). Jesus gave up his heavenly home, his power, and his glory, and out of his love, took on the flesh of a human. He was born of a virgin among the lowly animals and chose to live in this fallen world, troubled by evil and human suffering. Jesus gave so much of his time to those who sought him that he had little time for himself. Still, he was rejected by many he came to redeem. He never expressed regret or complained about this human experience but taught us what is possible when we accept God's love and put our trust in God's saving grace.

Jesus did not just teach us, but he put his words into action. He chose to lay down his life by way of the cross, letting us know that life and death are in God's hands. In this genuine act of laying down his life on the cross, Jesus took our place and paid our sin debt. He demonstrated to us that if we try to save our life, we will lose it, but if we lose it for the sake of the kingdom of God, we will find it (Matt. 10:39). Thus, God's plan to offer sinners eternal life, through His Son, Jesus Christ, who knew no sin, was fulfilled. God, through Christ, was reconciling the world to Himself. Christ not only laid down his life on the cross for our great spiritual healing of salvation, but he also did so for the healing of our minds, our bodies, and our relationships. The early church understood healing as a major part of God's redemptive plan of salvation. Salvation and healing are two sides of the same coin, and biblically, they go together. They are both rooted in God's love. Healing is in the atonement. (See Isa. 42; 53; 61; 2 Cor. 1:10; John 1:29; Acts 8:32; 1 Cor. 5:7.)

DEVOTION

Almighty God, when I read the account of the townsfolk bringing all their sick to the healing Christ, am I doing my part in caring for the wellbeing of the elderly? Am I among the townspeople who care about the sick and suffering? Forgive me when I am only concerned about my own needs and well-being.

Forgive your church, the body of Christ, who are often divided and confused concerning whether healing is still valid for today, while the sick and demon-possessed are neglected. Help us, Lord, to be your healing instruments, to bring healing, wholeness, and salvation to this broken and sin-sick world. Amen.

JOURNALING

To prepare for the next study, read Mark 1:40-45 and complete the questions for Healing Moment Three. Please pray for the participants and facilitators. Be prepared to have a lively discussion.

How is God calling you to respond to the sick in your family, on your job, in the church, and in your community?

JESUS IDENTIFIES WITH HUMAN BROKENNESS

§

CONTEMPLATION

The healing of the Leper tells us more about the compassion of Jesus than any other healing miracle found in the four gospels. For Jesus, touching the leper superseded the ceremonial rituals commanded by the law of Moses. In touching the leprous man, Mark allows us to see into the very heart and compassion of Jesus. His touch removed any doubts and fears the man may have had and reassured him of Jesus' willingness to heal him. Jesus' touch did not just heal the man physically, but healed him emotionally, and spiritually at the very core of his being. (See Lev. 13:1-3.) Jesus risked becoming ceremonially unclean to heal the leper. In putting his hands on the leper, in a real sense, Jesus identified with his humanity, as well as with his sins and disease. This man experienced God's love, mercy, and grace, revealed in the person of Jesus Christ. People are more important than man-made rules and laws.

BACKGROUND

According to the Hebrew scriptures, leprosy was thought to be an incurable disease sent from God as punishment for sin. A leper lived a difficult life. People with leprosy were considered outcasts and could not come within six feet of a healthy person, including their relatives. The movements of lepers were restricted by Jewish law. They had to wear torn clothes and let their hair grow long and loose. When they came near people, they were required to call out, "Unclean, unclean!"[1] They had to live outside the towns. This leper came and knelt before Jesus and begged him to make him clean. Perhaps he had heard that Jesus forgives sin, and being desperate, he took his chances, falling at his feet. The leper knew Jesus had the power to heal him, but he wavered in his faith, concerned whether Jesus would heal him. Seeing the man, Jesus was moved with compassion. As an act of compassion, Jesus reached out his hand, touched, and healed him. Jesus strictly ordered the man not to tell anyone, but to go and show himself to the priest, offering the sacrifice that Moses commanded for his cleansing, as a testimony to them. But the man went out telling everyone his story.

A HEALING MOMENT
Read Mark 1:40-45 from the NRSV or the NKJV.

NRSV
[40] *A leper came to him begging him, and kneeling he said to him, "If you choose, you can make me clean." [41] Moved with pity, Jesus stretched out his hand and touched him, and said to him, "I do choose. Be made clean!"[42] Immediately the leprosy left him, and he was made clean. [43] After sternly warning him he sent him away at once, [44] saying to him, "See that you say nothing to anyone; but go, show yourself to the priest, and offer for your cleansing what Moses commanded, as a testimony to them." [45] But he went out and began to proclaim it freely, and to spread the word, so that Jesus could no longer go into a town openly, but stayed out in the country; and people came to him from every quarter.*

NKJV

⁴⁰ Now a leper came to Him, imploring Him, kneeling to Him and saying to Him, "If You are willing, You can make me clean." ⁴¹ Then Jesus, moved with compassion, stretched out His hand and touched him, and said to him, "I am willing; be cleansed." ⁴² As soon as He had spoken, immediately the leprosy left him, and he was cleansed. ⁴³ And He strictly warned him and sent him away at once, ⁴⁴ and said to him, "See that you say nothing to anyone; but go your way, show yourself to the priest, and offer for your cleansing those things which Moses commanded, as a testimony to them." ⁴⁵ However, he went out and began to proclaim it freely, and to spread the matter, so that Jesus could no longer openly enter the city, but was outside in deserted places; and they came to Him from every direction.

DISCOVERY

1. What do the leper's words and gestures communicate to Jesus about his urgent desire to be healed?

2. If leprosy makes a person ceremonially unclean, why do you think Jesus felt it was necessary to touch the leper before healing him?

3. From the leper's point of view, make a list of the significance of Jesus' touching him.

4. How was Jesus' method of healing the leper shocking to the leper, to the disciples, and to those who witnessed it?

5. The prophet Isaiah tells us that a servant of the Lord *"has borne our infirmities and carried our diseases" (Isa. 53:4a).* Do you think Jesus may have had this prophecy in the back of his mind when he touched the leper? Explain.

ENCOURAGEMENT

When I was growing up in my hometown of Roanoke, Virginia, there was an old man of small stature whose speech was barely intelligible. He lacked social skills and wore his shoes on the wrong feet. Some people made fun of him, calling him insulting names and treating him as an outcast. His family tried to protect him by isolating him from the public. Like the leper, he too had been marginalized by a segment of society. Mark's account of the healing of the leper reminds us that God does not see or treat people as the world does. He sees them as precious and valued. Therefore, Jesus treated all who came to him for help with respect and dignity. Jesus championed the cause of broken humanity.

Both the Old and the New Testaments declare that God identifies with the poor, needy, orphans, and widows, who in most cases have been rejected by society. As the Messiah of God, Jesus championed the cause of all the oppressed. Jesus made it clear that those who followed him were to do the work that he had done. Like him, Jesus' disciples were to show mercy to the poor and needy. Their deeds would not go unnoticed but would be personally rewarded by him who will judge all nations. Conversely, those who refuse to show mercy toward the oppressed will receive eternal punishment. God shows concern for all the oppressed (Ps. 41; Prov. 14:31; 22:9; Matt. 25:32- 46). The good that God has shown to each of us is to be shown to those who are powerless or helpless. We are to care for those God cares about.

In the final judgment, when the Son of Man comes in his glory, he will gather all the nations and judge their deeds. Those who claim to be his disciples are expected to serve the least of these, as he has done. Everyone will be judged by God's standard of love—love of God and love of neighbor. Jesus summarized God's commandments as these two. God's standard of love puts everyone on a level playing field. As human beings, we will be judged not by what we have accumulated in this life, but by how we have used our resources to bless those in need. We have been blessed to be a blessing to others.

The prophet Zechariah reveals that God has blessed his people to be instruments of blessing to others (Zech. 8:13). We are Christ's hands, feet, and voice. Jesus told his disciples that he did not come to be served, but to serve. As his disciples, we too are called to serve in Christ's name. The writer of Hebrews tells us that God works through our salvation by signs, wonders, miracles, and gifts of the Holy Spirit. This means that our salvation is not static but becomes a living witness that Christ is in residence in our lives. Our salvation becomes tangible and visible by our sacrificial service to others in Christ's name. (See Heb. 2:1-4.)

As the body of Christ, we are to continue Christ's kingdom work. Jesus made this claim: *"People who are well do not need a doctor, but only those who are sick. I have not come to call respectable people, but outcasts"* (Mark 2:17, GNT). As Christ's followers, we are to care for those who are left to fend for themselves when they do not have the resources to do so.

REACTION

6. Do your words and deeds conform to God's standard of loving your neighbor as you love yourself?

7. Under what circumstance have you humbled yourself before Jesus?

8. When Jesus looked at the leper and touched him, did he see his humanity before he saw his diseased condition?

9. When you minister to others in Christ's name, how has Jesus' treatment of the leper informed you concerning how to pray for the sick and oppressed?

10. In Jesus day, society called lepers unclean and ostracized them. What did Jesus convey to society—and to us—by touching the leper?

11. Describe what you will take away from this Healing Moment that has helped to change your perspective about those who are marginalized today?

GOING DEEPER

Human touch can be either a powerful expression of love or a humiliating and harmful gesture. Jesus showed us that human touch is love in action. Touch, motivated by *agape* love, is both therapeutic and transformative. The desire to be touched is an inborn trait. Human touch is both beneficial and necessary to our well-being, an integral part of the human make-up.

Research shows that touch has many health benefits, including our physiological and psychological well-being. Touch reduces stress, lowers harmful cholesterol, and provides positive stimulation to the brain, producing beneficial hormones and giving us a sense of peace and wellness. A lack of touch is pathogenic, producing the opposite health and psychological benefits.[2] Love compels us to touch others. Human touch communicates compassion, caring, hope, acceptance, and a sense of belonging. These are godly deeds of *agape love.*

DEVOTION

Heavenly Father, thank you for not despising your sinful and broken humanity. Thank you for loving and caring for your creation, even when we are unlovable. Thank you for loving me just the way I am. Thank you for sending us a Savior who demonstrated your love to all, especially to those whom society has made invisible and non-human. Lord, show me the way of love that I might lift those who have been kicked to the curb by society. When I look the other way or do nothing, I am siding with those who do wrong. Forgive me when I act indifferent to those who need your help the most. Help me to remember that when I do good or evil to the least of these, I am doing it to you. Amen.

JOURNALING

To prepare for the next study, read Mark 2:1-12 and complete the questions for Healing Moment Four. Please pray for the participants and facilitators. Be prepared to have a lively discussion.

Picture Jesus, touching you and looking at you with love and compassion. Whom do you know that God is calling you to pull out of the shadows of society? What will your response be?

THE HEALING POWER
OF FORGIVENESS

§

CONTEMPLATION

Forgiveness is a powerful way to experience healing that may otherwise elude us. The healing of the paralytic gives us hope that forgiveness is possible. In forgiving the paralytic of his sins, Jesus opened the way for him to experience God's amazing grace. The Pharisees and scribes had a head knowledge of the Jewish sabbath law but knew nothing about grace. Understanding grace requires heart knowledge—spiritual knowledge. They did get one thing right— only God can forgive sins. However, they failed to see the incarnation of God manifested in the words and deeds of Jesus Christ. In the healing of the paralytic, they failed to see a demonstration of the power of grace. Forgiveness is a gracious gift that opens the way to all wholeness, and ultimately, to salvation.

BACKGROUND

Jesus barely had time to catch his breath before another human situation confronted him, demanding his time and attention. Jesus was unflappable because he knew it was for this reason he had come—to atone for human sin.

The healing of the paralytic is a unique and powerful healing story of divine grace. It is also a demonstration of faith and deeds in action. Mark has shown us over and over that Jesus Christ looks for every opportunity to connect God's power with human needs. Luke's version of this same healing incident tells us that God's power was strongly with Jesus to heal (Luke 5: 17). Christ looks beyond our faults and sees our needs. Mark revealed that God works through ordinary people who put their faith into action. This is one of those stories that miracles are made of.

A HEALING MOMENT
Read Mark 2:1-12 from the NRSV or the NKJV.

NRSV

When he returned to Capernaum after some days, it was reported that he was at home. ² *So many gathered around that there was no longer room for them, not even in front of the door; and he was speaking the word to them.*³ *Then some people came, bringing to him a paralyzed man, carried by four of them.* ⁴ *And when they could not bring him to Jesus because of the crowd, they removed the roof above him; and after having dug through it, they let down the mat on which the paralytic lay.* ⁵ *When Jesus saw their faith, he said to the paralytic, "Son, your sins are forgiven."* ⁶ *Now some of the scribes were sitting there, questioning in their hearts, "Why does this fellow speak in this way? It is blasphemy! Who can forgive sins but God alone?"* ⁸ *At once Jesus perceived in his spirit that they were discussing these questions among themselves; and he said to them, "Why do you raise such questions in your hearts?* ⁹*Which is easier, to say to the paralytic, 'Your sins are forgiven,' or to say, 'Stand up and take your mat and walk?'*

[10] But so that you may know that the Son of Man has authority on earth to forgive sins"—he said to the paralytic— [11]"I say to you, stand up, take your mat and go to your home." [12] And he stood up, and immediately took the mat and went out before all of them; so that they were all amazed and glorified God, saying, "We have never seen anything like this!"

NKJV

And again, He entered Capernaum after some days, and it was heard that He was in the house. [2] Immediately many gathered together, so that there was no longer room to receive them, not even near the door. And He preached the word to them. [3] Then they came to Him, bringing a paralytic who was carried by four men. [4] And when they could not come near Him because of the crowd, they uncovered the roof where He was. So, when they had broken through, they let down the bed on which the paralytic was lying.

When Jesus saw their faith, He said to the paralytic, "Son, your sins are forgiven you." [6] And some of the scribes were sitting there and reasoning in their hearts, "Why does this Man speak blasphemies like this? Who can forgive sins but God alone?" [8]

But immediately, when Jesus perceived in His spirit that they reasoned thus within themselves, He said to them, "Why do you reason about these things in your hearts? [9] Which is easier, to say to the paralytic, 'Your sins are forgiven you,' or to say, 'Arise, take up your bed and walk'? [10] But that you may know that the Son of Man has power on earth to forgive sins"—He said to the paralytic, [11] "I say to you, arise, take up your bed, and go to your house." [12] Immediately he arose, took up the bed, and went out in the presence of them all, so that all were amazed and glorified God, saying, "We never saw anything like this!"

DISCOVERY

1. What lesson do the four men teach us about faith and servant ministry?

2. Why didn't someone at the house where Jesus was teaching make room for the paralytic to be brought inside to be healed?

3. Why wasn't Jesus put off by the commotion created by the four men tearing through the roof and letting down the paralytic man in front of him?

4. Does the healing of the paralytic suggest that all sickness is the result of sin?

5. Why is forgiveness essential to wholeness, freedom, and relationships?

6. Put yourself in the place of the person with paralysis. What do you hear and feel when Jesus says to you: "Son (daughter), your sins are forgiven"?

ENCOURAGEMENT

You might not know what it is like to be paralyzed, unable to comb your hair, to brush your teeth, to feed yourself, or even to button up your blouse. Being paralyzed is something we cannot understand unless we have experienced it or been dependent on others to help us meet life's daily challenges. Just imagine what it would be like to have lost the ability to walk or to move your arms.

Now imagine that you are the paralytic person in this story. You have four friends willing to carry you to Jesus. They believe that if they can get you to Jesus, he will heal you. The five of you pray, believing that God would give you your heart's desire. Even before you are let down through the roof in front of Jesus, you sense something wonderful is about to happen. Through the actions of your four friends, your life is about to be radically changed. God looks beyond your faults and sees your needs. Forgiveness is love in action.

Forgiveness is an expression of God's unconditional love, which is a combination of divine mercy and grace. Conversely, failure to forgive prevents the expression of God's unconditional love. The paralytic man experienced the power of love on two fronts: through the grace of forgiveness and through the four men's action of loving their neighbor. It was the action of the love of neighbor that initiated this healing miracle. What kind of neighbor are you? How lively is your faith? How do you understand the significance of the Great Commandment as defined by Jesus?

RESPONSE

7. What correlation does Jesus' forgiving the paralytic's sins have with the healing of his body?

8. Why do you think no one at the house offered to help the four friends get the paralyzed man to Jesus to be healed?

9. Is forgiveness something you struggle with, either to receive or to give? (Read Matthew 6:9-15; 1 John 1:9-10; James 5:16.)

10. Read these scripture passages: Psalm 103:12; Isa. 38:17; 43:25; Jer. 31:34; Mic. 7:9; Col. 2:13-14. How completely does God forgive repentant sinners?

11. Describe what you will take away from this Healing Moment that has helped to change your perspective about your understanding of forgiveness and how you will use it to walk in freedom and peace.

GOING DEEPER

For many people, forgiveness is one of the most confusing and misunderstood spiritual principles to practice. It is difficult because many people think it is a matter of the human will. Forgiving others or even ourselves is humanly challenging. Why? Forgiveness can only be achieved with God's help. God gives the repentant person the ability to forgive someone who has hurt or wronged him or her. This is called grace.

When we choose to forgive a person, who has hurt or wronged us, God fills our heart with His love, making forgiveness possible. As stated earlier, forgiveness is both an expression of grace and mercy. It releases God's power of grace to let go of the pain and hurt. It benefits both parties, freeing them of their wrongs. However, whether the other person accepts or rejects it, we are only responsible for forgiving. Forgiving the paralytic demonstrated the spiritual nature of healing. Through grace, God offered him divine mercy, which resulted in his healing.

The goal of forgiveness is always to lead to healing, reconciliation, and peace. However, because of the nature of sin and the complexity of the human personality, this does not always lead to the results that God intends.

DEVOTION

Loving and merciful God, thank You for sending Jesus Christ, who opened the way to your forgiving grace, which leads to healing, wholeness, and salvation. Forgiveness is an expression of your grace, mercy, and unconditional love. Thank You for looking beyond my faults and seeing my needs. Teach me how-to live-in love and harmony with you and with my neighbors. This is my humble prayer. Amen.

JOURNALING

To prepare for the next study, read Mark 3:1-6 and complete the questions for Healing Moment Five. Please pray for the participants and facilitators. Be prepared to have a lively discussion.

Ask the Holy Spirit to reveal a person or persons, including yourself, whom you need to forgive or ask for forgiveness. Jot down their names. If the person is deceased or you have lost contact, write a letter to that person, expressing your remorse and forgiveness. Pray, asking God to release you from guilt, shame, and hurt. Burn the letter as a way of releasing the person and as a means of closing this chapter in your life.

If the person you have wronged is living and lives near you, ask God to give you the strength, courage, and the opportunity to go to him or her and ask for forgiveness. Write down your thoughts and feelings. Pay attention to what you have discovered about yourself and God's amazing grace. Offer a prayer of thanksgiving and praise to God, that this situation is now done with and finished.

HEALING IS ALWAYS LAWFUL

§

CONTEMPLATION

People go to church or synagogue for different reasons. Most people go to church to offer their worship to God and to give thanks for God's love, goodness, mercy, and salvation through Jesus Christ. Some people go to church out of habit because that is what they have always done. Still others go to church because they want to be connected with their family and friends and to offer their service to God. Others go to church hoping that they will receive help and answers to their day-to-day challenges. Still others have found the church to be their only connection to God, which gives them a sense of meaning and purpose in their lives. There are a few people who go to church to be seen and heard. The Pharisees went to the synagogue on this sabbath, not to worship or to learn, but to spy on Jesus and accuse him of breaking the sabbath. Why do you go to church?

BACKGROUND

Mark tells us that on another sabbath, Jesus went into the synagogue as was his custom. His attention was drawn to a man with a withered hand. Some of the attendees watched him closely to see f he would heal the man on the sabbath. Jesus had the man stand up in front so that everyone could see him. Having their attention, Jesus asked them a profound question, *"Which is lawful on the sabbath: to do good or to do evil, to save life or to kill"(Mk. 3:4 NIV)?* Because the people remained silent, Jesus looked at them in anger and disgust.

A HEALING MOMENT
Read Mark 3:1-6 from the NSRV or the NKJV.

NRSV

Again, he entered the synagogue, and a man was there who had a withered hand. ²They watched him to see whether he would cure him on the sabbath, so that they might accuse him. ³ And he said to the man who had the withered hand, "Come forward." ⁴ Then he said to them, "Is it lawful to do good or to do harm on the sabbath, to save life or to kill?" But they were silent. ⁵ He looked around at them with anger; he was grieved at their hardness of heart and said to the man, "Stretch out your hand." He stretched it out, and his hand was restored. ⁶ The Pharisees went out and immediately conspired with the Herodians against him, how to destroy him.

NKJV

And He entered the synagogue again, and a man was there who had a withered hand. ² So they watched Him closely, whether He would heal him on the Sabbath, so that they might accuse Him. ³And He said to the man who had the withered hands, "Step forward." ⁴Then He said to them, "Is it lawful on the Sabbath to do good or to do evil, to save life or to kill?" but they kept silent. ⁵And when He had looked around at them with anger, being grieved by the hardness of their hearts, He said to the man, "Stretch out your hand." And he stretched it out, and his hand was restored as whole as the other. ⁶ Then the Pharisees went out and immediately plotted with the Herodians against Him, how they might destroy Him.

DISCOVERY

1. What made Jesus extremely upset with the people's response to his question concerning whether it was lawful to heal on the Sabbath?

2. How does the healing of the man with the withered hand differ from the previous four healings performed by Jesus?

3. Why do you think Jesus was more concerned with healing the man's withered hand than with being religiously correct?

4. How did Jesus challenge the paralyzed man's faith?

5. In what way did the miracles done on the sabbath challenge the religious leaders' literal interpretation of the sabbath and work done on the sabbath?

6. Read Mark 2:27-28. How does Jesus make his case that it is always lawful or right to do good works on the sabbath?

ENCOURAGEMENT

Mark wanted his readers to see the healing miracles as living proof that good triumphs over evil. The miracles of Jesus clearly show that all manifestations of human suffering are evil and must always be confronted and eradicated. Mark further revealed that demonic activity was the primary source of most human suffering and the evil in the world. Having made the connection between human suffering and evil, Jesus made the case that it is always justified and lawful to do good works on the sabbath. When Jesus confronted the people about working on the sabbath, their silence convinced him that the religious leaders were holding their tradition on a standard with God's Word.[1]

The Pharisees refused to believe Jesus was their Messiah, despite the miraculous signs he performed that were spoken of by their prophets. They felt threatened by his growing popularity. They saw Jesus only as a troublemaker. They were not open to being taught by this young Jewish upstart.

The Pharisees failed to understand God's original intent for the sabbath. They put the Mosaic law above the needs of people, thus turning the sabbath, intended as a blessing, into a curse. Freedom was turned into bondage. Righteousness became self-righteousness. Hope became despair. The keeping of the law became idolatry.

The Pharisees had forgotten that their Hebrew scriptures instructed them concerning the love of neighbor. Because they were so removed from their Scriptures and bent on practicing their man-made rules, they were willing to perpetuate human suffering, allowing the evil work of Satan to go unchallenged.[2] They would rather have this man remain in his handicapped condition than to see him well, living a productive life, providing for his family, and making a positive contribution to society.

Trying to maintain the status quo, the Pharisees failed to connect the dots between the miracles and the power and authority Jesus possessed, which revealed the presence of God.[3] Although

God's laws are important, they were never meant to be elevated above the good of humankind, and God's laws were not intended to be used to disregard God's mercy and grace that the sabbath was created for.[4]

Recognizing the hardness of their hearts, Jesus realized the Pharisees had not only rejected him as their Messiah, but they were also rejecting God's salvation that he had come to bring to Israel and the world. This is what angered Jesus the most. Jesus exposed their hearts and minds, showing that they were more loyal to their religious system than to God's acts of mercy and grace.[5]

To correct their wrong thinking, Jesus reminded them that the sabbath was made for man and not man made for the sabbath (Mark 2:27-28). Rather than change, the Pharisees were more determined to kill Jesus and to rid themselves of what they considered to be a troublemaker.

RESPONSE

7. What religious tradition do you practice that puts you at odds with Jesus Christ and God's kingdom work?

8. What was really behind the Pharisees' attitude of wanting to kill Jesus for doing good on the sabbath?

9. Why is healing always lawful on the sabbath?

10. What was Jesus communicating to the Pharisees when he said, "The Son of Man is the Lord of the sabbath"?

11. Describe what you will take away from this Healing Moment that has helped to change your perspective about your view of the sabbath law handed down by Moses?

GOING DEEPER

The healing miracles of Jesus revealed that human suffering and evil are more common than people would like to admit. Mark has shown that suffering and evil co-exist and are subtle and ambiguous. They are like bookends in the day-to-day challenges of life. However, Jesus recognized their destructive nature and potential for causing human despair. Sickness and disease were not originally a part of God's good creation.

Human suffering was introduced through the sin of disobedience of the first human family. Jesus recognized there was a subtle or hidden evil presence working in the world, twenty-four/seven. Jesus' healing miracles demonstrated that God's kingdom had broken into the human realm. It also reveals that Satan's kingdom in the world is being dismantled.

In John's gospel, Jesus contrasts the work of Satan from his kingdom work: *"The thief comes only to steal and kill and destroy; I have come that they might have life, and have it to the full" (John 10:10 NIV).* Jesus refers to the thief as Satan. Jesus Christ came to restore God's good creation—God's *shalom.*

The Hebrew word *shalom* can be translated as *prosperity, health, complete, wholeness, wellness, peace* or *to the full.* Jesus came to expose and to eradicate all forms of demonic activity and evil influence which are manifested in sickness, disease, sin, broken relationships, and death. Luke captures the essence of this:

> *The word which God sent to the children of Israel, preaching peace through Jesus Christ—He is Lord of all—that word you know, which was proclaimed throughout all Judea, and began from Galilee after the baptism which John preached: how God anointed Jesus of Nazareth with the Holy Spirit and with power, who went about doing good and healing all who were oppressed by the devil, for God was with Him (Acts 10:36-38, NKJV).*

DEVOTION

"Spirit of the Living God, fall afresh on me. Melt me, mold me, fill me, use me."[6] The songwriter clearly expresses my sentiments and desire to be filled with the presence and power of God. Help me to be conformed to your will and your ways and to live my life pleasing to you. Teach me to live as Jesus lived, to love as he loved, to pray as he prayed, and to serve as he served. When I fall short, help me to get up, dust myself off, and continue my service to the Lord, through serving others. Thank You for hearing my prayer! Amen.

JOURNALING

To prepare for the next study, read Mark 3:13-19 and complete the questions for Healing Moment Six. Please pray for the participants and facilitators. Be prepared to have a lively discussion.

In what way or ways do you interfere with your own wholeness or well-being? List them below. Seek the Holy Spirit's guidance and help to come up with a holistic plan to choose lifestyles that promote health and wholeness. Remember, it is possible to experience well-being at every stage of your life.

JESUS EMPOWERS HIS DISCIPLES TO HEAL

§

CONTEMPLATION

How cool would it be to have the opportunity to hang out with Jesus and spend time talking to him about life, ministry, service, faith, and the kingdom of God. This was an exciting time for the disciples to be with Jesus, learning how he approached ministry. What Jesus told them on that mountainside challenged their faith and changed their lives forever. Over time, they, with Jesus, would change the world for the good. Jesus trained, empowered, and used this ragtag group of men to continue his kingdom work after he had completed his earthly mission and returned to his heavenly Father. When that time came, Jesus' kingdom work would become the kingdom work of the disciples and those who would come after them.

BACKGROUND

Jesus invited his disciples to accompany him on a mountainside. There, he gave them an overview of the state of his ministry. They also discovered that Jesus had chosen them to share in his life and ministry—God's kingdom work. Jesus surprised them by appointing them as his apostles, symbolizing the twelve tribes of Israel. They would now have opportunities to get up close and personal in the day-to-day operation of his ministry. Their new status would be a game changer.

Before he sent them out, Jesus conferred his power and authority to them, which God had bestowed on him. The commissioning of this special group of twelve apostles represented the creation of the infant church (Eph. 2:20).

A HEALING MOMENT
Read Mark 3:13-19 from the NRSV or the NKJV.

NRSV
He went up the mountain and called to him those whom he wanted, and they came to him. [14] And he appointed twelve, whom he also named apostles, to be with him, and to be sent out to proclaim the message, [15] and to have authority to cast out demons. [16] So he appointed the twelve: Simon (to whom he gave the name Peter); [17] James son of Zebedee and John the brother of James (to whom he gave the name Boanerges, that is, Sons of Thunder);[18] and Andrew, and Philip, and Bartholomew, and Matthew, and Thomas, and James son of Alphaeus, and Thaddaeus, and Simon the Cananaean, [19] and Judas Iscariot, who betrayed him.

NKJV
[13] And He went up on the mountain and called to Him those He Himself wanted. And they came to Him. [14] Then He appointed twelve, that they might be with Him and that He might send them out to preach, [15] and to have power to heal sicknesses and to cast out demons: [16] Simon,[c] to whom He gave the name Peter; [17] James the son of Zebedee and John the brother of James, to whom He gave the name Boanerges, that is, "Sons of Thunder"; [18] Andrew, Philip, Bartholomew, Matthew, Thomas, James the son of Alphaeus, Thaddaeus, Simon the Cananite, [19] and Judas Iscariot, who also betrayed Him.

DISCOVERY

1. What were the apostles feeling and thinking when Jesus told them they would be sent out before him, to engage in his ministry of preaching and healing?

2. If you were invited to spend the day with Jesus, what would you talk to him about?

3. How much time do you spend with God, talking about the things that matter to God's kingdom work?

4. How have you responded to God's call to Christian discipleship— servant ministry?

5. What or who has helped prepare you to respond to God's call to servant ministry?

6. Is there a correlation between faith and obedience concerning your response to the call to Christian discipleship?

ENCOURAGEMENT

Probably no CEO in today's business world would have selected the twelve disciples. What set them apart from most people was their love and total commitment to Jesus and his kingdom work. They saw something special in Jesus, and he saw something exceptional about them. Although they possessed all the human failures, weaknesses, and drives for ambition common to all of us, Jesus saw in them that they could become, not what they were.

Although at first, they had a difficult time grasping the significance of their call to servant ministry, they would eventually get it. Their kingdom work was a testimony to their faithfulness and obedience to Christ. The work they did is still making a difference and impacting the church and world. God uses ordinary people like you and me. Are you up to the challenge?

RESPONSE

7. Do you accept the premise that you can make a difference in the kingdom work of God? Why? Why not?

8. Have you responded to God's call to follow Christ in advancing the work of the kingdom?

9. Take a moment and think about your call to servant ministry. Using a scale from 1 to 5, with 5 being the effective side of ministry, how would you grade the effectiveness of your servant ministry?

10. Read John 14:12. In what way does this statement of Jesus inform your Christian service?

11. Do you believe that one person can make a difference in the kingdom work of God?

GOING DEEPER

During the last days of Jesus' earthly ministry, he told several parables. Jesus told the Parable of the Talents to teach the disciples an important lesson about being diligent in doing God's will while they wait for his return. In the parable, Jesus is the man, and his disciples are his servants. His property is the mission of God's kingdom. The man entrusted his property to three of his servants. To one servant he gave five talents, to another two talents, and the third he gave one talent. The man went on a long journey. While he was away, the servant with the five talents at once went out and made some deals and earned five more talents. The servant with the two talents did the same and earned two additional talents. The servant with the one talent buried his talent in the ground because he was afraid he might make a bad investment and lose the man's talent.

When the man returned, he called the servants to see what they had done with his talents. He heard the good news that the servants with the five and two talents had doubled the man's talents. This pleased the man, and he rewarded the two servants. The servant who buried his one talent gave it back to the owner. He was punished because he was irresponsible and untrustworthy.

All born again believers have received different talents, gifts, abilities, and possessions, entrusted to them by God. Each of us is responsible for using these possessions in ways that promote the kingdom of God. God is counting on each of us to use the talents, abilities, and gifts faithfully and obediently we have been given to advance God's kingdom. Have you been a good steward of God's gifts to advance the kingdom?

Each of us is responsible not only to discover our gifts but to develop and use our gifts wisely. How we use our gifts can make an eternal difference in God's kingdom. What we do for God has eternal consequences. When you meet the Lord at the end of the age when your work on this earth is finished, do you want to hear these words from the Lord: "*Well done, good and faithful servant; you were faithful over a few things, I will make you ruler over many things. Enter into the joy of your lord*" (Matt. 25:21 NIV; 2 Kings 10:30; Mark 7:37).

DEVOTION

Gracious God, I give you thanks and praise for your many gifts. Thank you for counting me worthy to participate with Christ in advancing your kingdom work. Help me to use the gifts, talents, and abilities you have entrusted to me to build up the body of Christ, to transform the world. May all that I do in Christ's name bring you honor, glory, and praise. Amen.

JOURNALING

To prepare for the next study, read Mark 5:1-20 and complete the questions for Healing Moment Seven. Please pray for the participants and facilitators. Be prepared to have a lively discussion.

Make a list of the gifts you have received. Describe how each of the gifts could be used to bring about healing to a broken and sinful world.

JESUS' POWER KNOWS NO BOUNDS

§

CONTEMPLATION

The word supreme perfectly characterizes who Jesus Christ is. It means the highest in rank and authority. Mark's gospel constantly makes the point that the demonic realm recognized the *supreme* power and authority of Jesus:

> *When he saw Jesus from a distance, he ran and bowed down before him; and he shouted at the top of his voice, "What have you to do with me, Jesus, Son of the Highest God? I adjure you by God, do not torment me"* (Mark 5:7 NRSV).

Demons hate God and are an ever-present enemy of Jesus. They bow down not in worship of Jesus, but in respect and submission to his authority over them. Demons knew that Jesus had come to destroy them. They begged him not to do them harm or to send them out of the area. They knew their end was near.

BACKGROUND

The next three healing miracles in chapter five are significant and move Jesus' ministry to a higher spiritual level. Mark emphasized Jesus' supreme power and authority over demons, sickness, and now, death. We will consider each of the three healing incidents separately, in the order that Mark recorded them. The healing of Jairus's daughter and the woman with the bleeding problem will be addressed in the next Healing Moment.

Jesus' ministry moved beyond the territory of the Jews to a place called Gerasenes, a Gentile region where a small group of Jews lived. In Gerasenes, Jesus encountered another situation involving an exorcism of a man with an unclean spirit. The demons restrained the man in a cemetery among the tombs; he was at their mercy. The presence of a legion of demons in the man gave him super-human strength. No human could restrain the man, not even with iron shackles and chains. This shows that even the community was under the control of the demons.

A HEALING MOMENT
Read Mark 5:1-20 from NRSV or the NKJV.

NRSV

They came to the other side of the sea, to the country of the Gerasenes.² And when he had stepped out of the boat, immediately a man out of the tombs with an unclean spirit met him. ³ He lived among the tombs; and no one could restrain him anymore, even with a chain; ⁴ for he had often been restrained with shackles and chains, but the chains he wrenched apart, and the shackles he broke in pieces; and no one had the strength to subdue him.⁵ Night and day among the tombs and on the mountains he was always howling and bruising himself with stones. ⁶ When he saw Jesus from a distance, he ran and bowed down before him; ⁷ and he shouted at the top of his voice, "What have you to do with me, Jesus, Son of the Most High

God? I adjure you by God, do not torment me." [8] For he had said to him, "Come out of the man, you unclean spirit!" [9] Then Jesus asked him, "What is your name?" He replied, "My name is Legion; for we are many." [10] He begged him earnestly not to send them out of the country. [11] Now there on the hillside a great herd of swine was feeding; [12] and the unclean spirits begged him, "Send us into the swine; let us enter them." [13] So he gave them permission. And the unclean spirits came out and entered the swine; and the herd, numbering about two thousand, rushed down the steep bank into the sea, and were drowned in the sea.[14]

The swineherds ran off and told it in the city and in the country. Then people came to see what it was that had happened. [15] They came to Jesus and saw the demoniac sitting there, clothed and in his right mind, the very man who had had the legion; and they were afraid. [16] Those who had seen what had happened to the demoniac and to the swine reported it. [17] Then they began to beg Jesus to leave their neighborhood. [18] As he was getting into the boat, the man who had been possessed by demons begged him that he might be with him. [19] But Jesus refused, and said to him, "Go home to your friends, and tell them how much the Lord has done for you, and what mercy he has shown you." [20] And he went away and began to proclaim in the Decapolis how much Jesus had done for him; and everyone was amazed.

NKJV

Then they came to the other side of the sea, to the country of the Gadarenes.[2] And when He had come out of the boat, immediately there met Him out of the tombs a man with an unclean spirit, [3] who had his dwelling among the tombs; and no one could bind him, not even with chains, [4] because he had often been bound with shackles and chains. And the chains had been pulled apart by him, and the shackles broken in pieces; neither could anyone tame him. [5] And always, night and day, he was in the mountains and in the tombs, crying out and cutting himself with stones. ⁶ When he saw Jesus from afar, he ran and worshiped Him. ⁷ And he cried out with a loud voice and said, "What have I to do with You, Jesus, Son of the Most High God? I implore You by God that You do not torment me." ⁸ For He said to him, "Come out of the man, unclean spirit!" ⁹ Then He asked him, "What is your name?" And he answered, saying, "My name is Legion; for we are many. " 10 Also he begged Him earnestly that He would not send them out of the country. ¹¹ Now a large herd of swine was feeding there near the mountains. ¹² So all the demons begged Him, saying, "Send us to the swine, that we may enter them." ¹³ And at once Jesus gave them permission. Then the unclean spirits went out and entered the swine (there were about two thousand); and the herd ran violently down the steep place into the sea, and drowned in the sea. ¹⁴ So those who fed the swine fled, and they told it in the city and in the country. And they went out to see what it was that had happened. ¹⁵ Then they came to Jesus, and saw the one who had been demon-possessed and had the legion, sitting and clothed and in his right mind. And they were afraid. ¹⁶ And those who saw it told them how it happened to him who had been demon-possessed, and about the swine. ¹⁷ Then they began to plead with Him to depart from their region. ¹⁸ And when He got into the boat, he who had been demon-possessed begged Him that he might be with Him. ¹⁹ However, Jesus did not permit him, but said to him, "Go home to your friends, and tell them what great things the Lord has done for you, and how He has had compassion on you." ²⁰ And he departed and began to proclaim in Decapolis all that Jesus had done for him; and all marveled.

DISCOVERY

1. Demons recognized Jesus as the Son of the Most High God. What prevented the leaders and the people from recognizing who Jesus is, even after observing his miracle-working power and authority over demons?

2. Why did the demons beg Jesus not to send them out of the area?

3. In what ways were the demons in control of the community and what was the significance?

4. What does the farming of pigs tell you about this region and the Jews living there?

5. Jesus had now moved his mission to a Gentile territory outside of Galilee. Why is this significant?

6. When the demon saw Jesus and bowed down before him, was this an act of worship of him?

ENCOURAGEMENT

Mark shows that oppression by demons was not only widespread, but their reach and influence went beyond ethnic, territorial boundaries, and the social status of people. The fact that Jesus' mission is being extended to the Gentiles suggests that the good news of salvation is to be preached to all nations (Mark 13:10; 14:9). The good news is that Jesus has come to set the captives free. He has come to give people victory over evil, sin, and death. Jesus has come to give believers power not only to overcome Satan but to empower God's people to release others from demonic activity. Salvation is God's response to sin. The path to victory over sin and death is salvation. Jesus enables believers to live a life free of the desire to sin, always living with the cross before us. The cross is our motivation to live lives pleasing to the Lord, Jesus Christ, for what he has done for us.

God sent Jesus to help people experience wholeness in every aspect of life, which includes spirit, body, mind (emotions), and relationships. This is the abundant life Jesus came to bring. Jesus sent the Holy Spirit to empower

God's people are to live victorious lives. Our part is to choose lifestyles that promote well-being in every stage of life. All of this is possible only by living the Spirit-filled life. Do you want to live the life that God intends for you to live?

RESPONSE

7. What did the demon-possessed man learn about the severity of his condition after Jesus permitted the demons to enter the pigs?

8. How did Mark describe the mental condition of the man before and after Jesus healed him?

9. Read Luke 9:1-2; 10:9; 17-20. Describe what Jesus wanted the disciples to understand about the authority they had over demons.

10. Is there a connection between the healing of the man and the drowning of the pigs?

11. By allowing the demons to enter the pigs, Jesus was illustrating something significant he wanted all the spectators to comprehend. What was illustrated in their very eyes that told the whole story of the coming kingdom of God?

GOING DEEPER

Mark made it clear that Jesus fully understood his primary mission was to proclaim a message of the Kingdom of God—salvation to the Jewish people. Despite the opposition and challenges that confronted his mission, he is not discouraged or distracted. As we observe Jesus' kingdom work, it becomes increasingly clear that he is passionate about liberating all people from their suffering and bondage. Jesus gives this kingdom work to the church to continue after he returns to his Father. His last instruction to his followers was to proclaim the good news of the gospel of salvation—first, in our homes, then to our friends and acquaintances, next to our community, and finally to the world. (See Matt.28:18-20; Acts 1:5-8.)

The gospel of salvation is not a message about a set of laws, or dos and don'ts. The gospel of salvation is about covenant relationships with the Creator. Salvation is offered to the whole world. (See John 3:16.) Jesus' death on the cross has impacted the whole world. Jesus did not only proclaim the gospel of salvation; he demonstrated it through the miracles he performed and the lives he touched and transformed.

Jesus changed the life of the demon-possessed man he had just healed. Notice that Jesus did not silence the man from telling others what God had done for him. He said to him go home (to his Gentile neighbors) and tell his family and friends *"how much the Lord has done for you, and what mercy he has shown you"* (Mk. 5:19). As he did so, the people in Decapolis learned about the goodness of God, and everyone was amazed. Gentiles have now experienced the love and healing grace of God. How many family members and friends have you told what Jesus has done for you? God's goodness toward us is meant to be shared with others.

Mark made it transparently clear in this healing action that the demons not only had control of this man but also held the community hostage. Mark pointed out that this was not just an individual problem, but a community dilemma. The community seemed powerless to help this man to reclaim his wholeness and place in his family and the community. The man and the community seemed blind to the kingdom resources they had through Jesus Christ, their Messiah. Rather than experiencing God's liberating power through Jesus Christ, members of the faith community were wringing their hands in fear and defeat.

Those in the religious community were at a loss as to what their role should be. Rather than protect and liberate their weakest members, all they could do was isolate, bind, and guard people. The faith community believed it was subjected to the power of Satan's demons.[1] When we reject God's salvation, we become confused about our place and purpose in the work of God. Satan seeks to perpetuate this lie and to keep God's people confused and bound.

Satan becomes freer to go around, seeking whom he may devour (1 Peter 5:8-9). His three-fold task is to steal, kill, and destroy (John 10:10). Notice that the infestation of the man was controlled by a legion of demons. The demons approached Jesus because they did not want him to interfere with their control over their victim and the community.

Although the demons recognized Jesus' divinity and bowed down to him, they did it out of respect and not out of reverence for him. They were trying to protect themselves and their turf. Referring to themselves as legion, the demons were trying to gain power over Jesus. They requested that Jesus not send them outside of the area, but instead, into the pigs. Surprisingly, Jesus permitted them to go into the pigs. What happened next is just as surprising.

Jesus spoke to the demons just as he had spoken to the wind and the sea. Each of them had to obey the power and authority of God's Spirit. The good news is God sent us a Messiah to restore our place and purpose in God's kingdom that was lost in the Fall. Mark showed the faith community that God's people had been empowered with the same authority demonstrated by Jesus in casting out the unclean spirits from the man living among the tombs.

When Jesus healed the man, he regained control of his mind. Having his mind renewed, he took off his unclean, tattered clothes, washed himself, and put on clean clothes. When the people saw his transformation, the community discovered they did not have to live in the bondage of Satan. They also discovered they had to turn to Jesus to be changed like this man. This is the message of the gospel, demonstrated through all the healing miracles.

DEVOTION

Healing Christ, help me recognize your divine presence and worship you for who you are. May your name be praised, and your kingdom come into my life, on earth as in heaven. Thank you for demonstrating the transforming power of God into my life. Because of what you have done for me, I don't have to live in fear or bondage. Loving God, thank you for your providential care. In Jesus' name! Amen.

JOURNALING

To prepare for the next study, read Mark 5:25-34 and complete the questions for Healing Moment Eight. Please pray for the participants and facilitators. Be prepared to have a lively discussion.

Write in your journal a list of how much God has done for you and the mercy he has shown you.

HEALING MOMENT EIGHT
A FAITH THAT WOULD NOT BE DENIED

§

CONTEMPLATION

The thought of an incurable disease or death can be upsetting for many people. For some, the words *cancer* and *incurable* can be perceived as a death sentence. Even when I go to the doctor's office for my annual physical checkup, my blood pressure is always higher than normal. Just being in a doctor's office becomes unsettling. After the doctor's visit, my blood pressure returns to its normal level. As a young child, I had several bad experiences receiving medical care in a hospital and a doctor's office. I have tried to deal with this issue most of my adult life, but it persists.

The woman with a menstrual bleeding problem had many bad experiences with numerous doctors as she sought a cure for her serious health condition. She had spent all the money she had on doctors, but her condition got worse. We should count our blessings for what we have and don't have.

BACKGROUND

Jesus was back in a predominantly Jewish territory. He and his disciples had just stepped out of the boat onto the beach and were surrounded by a large crowd. Some had come to see what Jesus would do next. However, some in the crowd had come to be healed by him. Many of their circumstances were desperate because they were facing a life and death situation.

Time was not on their side. They needed a blessing and breakthrough from heaven! They needed a miracle! They needed to be healed by Jesus Christ, and time was running out.

A HEALING MOMENT
Read Mark 5:25-34 from NRSV or the NKJV.

NRSV
25 Now there was a woman who had been suffering from hemorrhages for twelve years. 26 She had endured much under many physicians and had spent all that she had; and she was no better, but rather grew worse. 27 She had heard about Jesus and came up behind him in the crowd and touched his cloak, 28 for she said, "If I but touch his clothes, I will be made well." 29 Immediately her hemorrhage stopped; and she felt in her body that she was healed of her disease 30Immediately aware that power had gone forth from him, Jesus turned about in the crowd and said: "Who touched my clothes?" 31 And his disciples said to him, "You see the crowd pressing in on you; how can you say, 'Who touched me?'" 32 He looked all around to see who had done it. 33 But the woman, knowing what had happened to her, came in fear and trembling, fell before him, and told him the whole truth. 34 He said to her, "Daughter, your faith has made you well; go in peace, and be healed of your disease."

NKJV
25 Now a certain woman had a flow of blood for twelve years, 26 and had suffered many things from many physicians. She had spent all that she had and was no better, but rather grew worse. 27 When she heard about Jesus, she came behind Him in the crowd and touched His garment. 28 For she said: "If only I may touch His clothes, I shall

be made well." ²⁹ Immediately the fountain of her blood was dried up, and she felt in her body that she was healed of the affliction. ³⁰ And Jesus, immediately knowing in Himself that power had gone out of Him, turned around in the crowd and said, "Who touched My clothes?" ³¹ But His disciples said to Him, "You see the multitude thronging You, and You say, 'Who touched Me?'" ³² And He looked around to see her who had done this thing. ³³ But the woman, fearing and trembling, knowing what had happened to her, came and fell before Him and told Him the whole truth. ³⁴ And He said to her, "Daughter, your faith has made you well. Go in peace, and be healed of your affliction."

DISCOVERY

1. Who or what do you turn to when you are faced with a health crisis requiring immediate action?

2. Think of a situation when your faith seemed smaller than the problem you faced. To whom did you turn?

3. Where did the woman's first glimmer of hope come from, turning her sorrow and disappointment into hope and a joyful expectation?

4. Why would Jesus spend so much time with this woman when Jairus's daughter was facing a life and death crisis?

5. What scripture comes to mind that gives you assurance God cares about the situations you face in your daily life?

6. What other challenges did the woman face that threatened the quality of her life?

ENCOURAGEMENT

So far, each of the healing incidents we have read about in Mark's gospel has common threads running through them. Each of the incidents varies in degree and length of human pain and suffering. Each of them has the potential to diminish the person's quality of life. The most important thread that runs through each is the depth of God's care and concern for His children, and assurance we are not alone in facing life's problems and challenges. No matter who came to Jesus for help, or the situation he or she was facing, Jesus always made each person's problem a high priority, no matter what else was going on. The psalmist got it right: *"God is our refuge and strength, an very-present help in trouble"* (Ps. 46:1 NIV). The healing miracles performed by Jesus demonstrate that the cares and needs of ordinary people matter to God. The miracles are powerful proof that not only does God love us, but he has made provisions for our health, wholeness, and salvation through Jesus Christ.

Jairus's daughter and the woman with the issue of blood found the solutions to their healing needs in the person of Jesus Christ. The woman had heard secondhand stories about Jesus' power to heal. They became messages of hope and good news, strengthening and emboldening a faith within her that would not be denied. Do you know that God cares about you and you matter to God?

RESPONSE

7. How have the healing miracles helped to strengthen your faith to be healed?

8. What compelled the woman to confess to Jesus that she was the person who touched his clothes?

9. What did Jesus communicate to the woman by referring to her as "daughter"?

10. Recount a situation or circumstance in your life when you felt that, if God had not responded quickly to your need, you would not have made it.

11. Describe what you will take away from this Healing Moment that has helped you to face an uncertain future or a life threatening situation?

GOING DEEPER

Let's get one thing straight concerning how the woman with the bleeding condition was healed. Healing is not magic. There is no magical power in Jesus' clothes. Jesus is not a genie whom a person can touch and have their needs met. As we have said, healing is rooted in divine love. God's love cannot be manipulated by human desires or even human needs. Only genuine faith can release God's healing power. God's power is an expression of His love, grace, and mercy. The healing miracles confirm that God is not indifferent to human pain and suffering. If the truth be told, God hurts and suffers with His creation.

Does this mean that all our prayers or desires for healing will always have a positive outcome, as the individuals we have read about: the man possessed by unclean spirits, Peter's mother-in-law, the many people Jesus healed at Peter's home, Jairus's daughter, or the woman with the hemorrhage? Only God can answer that question. Only God knows why some people are healed, and others are not. What we do know is that God loves and cares for His creation.

How, when, and who are healed rests with God alone. If God is the healer, who are we to question God's motives. We can rest assured that every decision God makes on our behalf is always for our good. The Apostle Paul explains it this way: *"We know that all things work together for good for those who love God, who are called according to his purpose" (Rom. 8:28 NRSV).* We must keep this essential fact in mind. Healing is God's will, and Jesus has proven this over and over.

The cross is the ultimate proof that everyone who has trusted God for their healing and salvation will be answered in the affirmative. Only believers understand that healing is in the atonement. The cross of Christ assures these three things will be accomplished in the resurrection: (1) The blood of Christ will cover our sins for eternity, (2) sickness will be eliminated for eternity, and (3) death will be destroyed for eternity. Believers will live forever in God's presence, free from sin, sickness, and death. Through the cross and in the resurrection, God's love in Christ will ultimately triumph over sin, sickness, and death.

Keep this fact in mind. While we live in these mortal bodies, all healing is only temporary. Healed or not, all of us will die unless Christ comes first. What little suffering we will have to endure on this side of the veil is not worth mentioning because of the glory believers will share with Christ in God's eternal kingdom. God always had a divine plan for our healing, wholeness, and salvation. In fact, Jesus' Hebrew name is *Joshua,* which means salvation. Jesus came to bring healing, wholeness, and salvation. Healing will ultimately happen, but some of us may have to wait for the resurrection for it to be manifested.

DEVOTION

Gracious and Healing God, thank you for your salvation, which is an expression of your unconditional love, revealed in Christ Jesus. Help me to trust you when things don't always work out the way I want them to. Give me the courage and faith to know that all my physical and spiritual needs will be completely met through Jesus Christ in my eternal home in heaven. In Jesus' name, I pray. Amen.

JOURNALING

To prepare for the next study, read Mark 5:21-24, 35-43 and complete the questions for Healing Moment Nine. Please pray for the participants and facilitators. Be prepared to have a lively discussion.

How might God respond to your present situation—or that of a family member or a loved one—that would bring you peace?

JESUS' SUPREME POWER OVER DEATH

§

CONTEMPLATION

If you have ever experienced a life-threatening illness of one of your children, you know the agony Jairus was going through. As a parent, you will do whatever it takes to get the best possible help to make your child well again. To whom do you turn when you are desperate to get the help your child needs? Jairus was willing to put his daughter's life into the hands of the Great Physician—the Healing Messiah of God (Isa. 42:6-7). Who is the first person you seek out when facing a crisis in your life?

BACKGROUND

Jesus got into the boat with his disciples and left the territory of the Gentiles, crossing the sea of Galilee to a Jewish region. A great crowd gathered around him. A leader of a local synagogue named Jairus moved through the crowd and, seeing Jesus, fell at his feet in desperation. Jairus pleaded fervently with him to come to his house and lay his hands on his young child who was dying. Jairus seemed confident in Jesus' ability to save his daughter from her life-and-death struggle.

Without hesitation, Jesus followed Jairus and the group that accompanied him. On the way to Jairus's home, Jesus was met by another person in a life-and-death condition. Surprisingly, Jesus was not in a hurry to move on to Jairus's house but became engaged with a woman who had a terminal bleeding condition. She came up behind Jesus and touched his clothes. As she touched Jesus, the lives of two families were held between life and death. Jesus lived within the present moment, taking life as it came. He always gave his full attention to the person or situation facing him.

A HEALING MOMENT
Read Mark 5:21-24; 35-43 from the NRSV or the NKJV.

NRSV
21 When Jesus had crossed again in the boat to the other side, a great crowd gathered around him; and he was by the sea. 22 Then one of the leaders of the synagogue named Jairus came and, when he saw him, fell at his feet 23 and begged him repeatedly, "My little daughter is at the point of death. Come and lay your hands on her, so that she may be made well, and live." 24 So he went with him.

35 While he was still speaking, some people came from the leader's house to say, "Your daughter is dead. Why trouble the teacher any further?" 36 But overhearing what they said, Jesus said to the leader of the synagogue, "Do not fear, only believe." 37 He allowed no one to follow him except Peter, James, and John, the brother of James. 38 When they came to the house of the leader of the synagogue, he saw a commotion, people weeping and wailing loudly. 39 When he had entered, he said to them, "Why do you make a commotion and weep? The child is not dead but sleeping." 40 And they laughed at him. Then he put them all outside, and took the child's father and mother and those who were with him, and went in where the child was. 41 He took her by the hand and said to her, "Talitha cum," which means, "Little girl, get up!" 42

And immediately the girl got up and began to walk about (she was twelve years of age). At this, they were overcome with amazement. ^{43} He strictly ordered them that no one should know this, and told them to give her something to eat.

NKJV

^{21} *Now when Jesus had crossed over again by boat to the other side, a great multitude gathered to Him, and He was by the sea. ^{22} And behold, one of the rulers of the synagogue came, Jairus by name. And when he saw Him, he fell at His feet ^{23} and begged Him earnestly, saying, "My little daughter lies at the point of death. Come and lay Your hands on her, that she may be healed, and she will live." ^{24} So Jesus went with him, and a great multitude followed Him and thronged Him.*

^{35} *While He was still speaking, some came from the ruler of the synagogue's house who said, "Your daughter is dead. Why trouble the Teacher any further?" ^{36} As soon as Jesus heard the word that was spoken, He said to the ruler of the synagogue, "Do not be afraid; only believe." ^{37} And He permitted no one to follow Him except Peter, James, and John the brother of James. ^{38} Then He came to the house of the ruler of the synagogue, and saw a tumult and those who wept and wailed loudly. ^{39} When He came in, He said to them, "Why make this commotion and weep? The child is not dead, but sleeping." ^{40} And they ridiculed Him. But when He had put them all outside, He took the father and the mother of the child, and those who were with Him, and entered where the child was lying. ^{41} Then He took the child by the hand, and said to her, "Talitha, cumi," which is translated, "Little girl, I say to you, arise." ^{42} Immediately the girl arose and walked, for she was twelve years of age. And they were overcome with great amazement. ^{43} But He commanded them strictly that no one should know it, and said that something should be given her to eat.*

DISCOVERY

1. How would you describe Jairus faith in Jesus' ability to heal his daughter, even in the face of death?

2. How would you describe expectant faith?

3. Describe a time when Jesus came through for you.

4. What makes you feel fearful and hopeless? Why?

5. How did Jesus respond to the news that Jairus's daughter had died?

6. As Christians, how should we respond when we receive bad news?

ENCOURAGEMENT

When the leaders of Jairus's home synagogue came, bearing the bad news that his daughter had died, Jesus said to them: *"Do not fear, only believe"* (Mk. 5:36). Jesus told Jairus (and he tells us) that nothing, absolutely nothing, is impossible to God. As Creator of all living things, God can certainly raise the dead.

In Jesus' conversation with Martha concerning the death of her brother, Lazarus, he encouraged her to believe her brother would rise from the dead. Martha thought Jesus was speaking about the end of the age when the saints of God will be raised in the resurrection. Jesus told her, *"Your brother will rise again. Martha said to him, I know that he will rise again in the resurrection on the last day." Jesus said to her, "I am the resurrection and the life. Those who believe in me, even though they die, will live, and everyone who lives and believes in me will never die"* (John 11:23-26 NSRV).

Each of these stories should give us hope for our resurrection. The resurrection stories should remove confusion and doubt concerning our eternal destiny with God. Mark wanted his readers to know for certain that the resurrection of the dead isn't hard for God. After all, if God is the creator of life, God certainly knows how to restore life and to sustain life.

RESPONSE

7. Is there any biblical support that informs believers in their expectation of the resurrection?

8. What did Jairus's daughter and the woman with the issue of blood have in common?

9. How are you to understand Jesus' use of the term sleeping when it refers to the dead?

10. Why did Jesus not allow the people at Jairus's house to accompany him in the room where he prayed for the dead girl? Explain.

11. Describe what you will take away from this Healing Moment that has helped to change your perspective about death or dying?

GOING DEEPER

You may have heard this saying in the Christian community: *"God may not be there when you want him, but He's always on time."* God is an on-time God. He has said many things that help us through difficult times and encourage us not to lose hope. I don't know of any situation or circumstance where Jesus did not offer people hope. The key word he used to build faith and to give hope was *believe.* To believe is to accept by faith the promises of God. We are not to waver in our faith concerning the promises of God. Healing is one of those promises.

Jesus challenged Jairus to believe and have faith in his ability to raise his daughter from the dead. Jesus offered Jairus hope and a promise. No matter what you are going through, God in Christ has the perfect solution. Many people miss their blessings because they are quick to give up. God, in Christ, has never made a promise He could not keep. One of the unique things Mark reveals about Jesus is that more often than not, he involved those he healed in their own healing miracle. Jesus does not want any person to feel hopeless or powerless. Jesus wants us to be a part of our solution, even when we don't know how things will turn out.

When we don't have the answers to our problems, Jesus admonishes us to be persistent in pursuing God's help, which builds faith. He tells us to *ask, seek, and knock: "Ask, and it will be given to you; seek, and you will find; knock, and it will be opened to you. For everyone who asks receives, and he who seeks finds, and to him who knocks it will be opened (Matt. 7:7-8 NKJV).*

DEVOTION

Healing God, thank you for sending your Son Jesus who is an expression of your love, compassion, mercy, and grace. This year, many of the members in our congregation have experienced the death of a loved one. Help us to know that when we face death or a life-threatening situation, we are not alone. May those who are mourning the death of a loved one know of Your comfort, presence, and peace. Turn their mourning into joy! In Jesus' name, I pray. Amen.

JOURNALING

To prepare for the next study, read Mark 6:7-13 and complete the questions for Healing Moment Ten. Please pray for the participants and facilitators. Be prepared to have a lively discussion.

What about death or dying concerns you the most? Read 1 Corinthians 15. Make notes about the hope, and assurance Paul gives concerning the resurrection from the dead.

HEALING MOMENT TEN

JESUS' DISCIPLES AS GOD'S HEALERS

§

CONTEMPLATION

Anyone who has taken seriously his or her call to servant ministry realizes it is hard and challenging. Why? The church has ill prepared the body of Christ concerning this important subject. Many Christian churches have not even taught one course on what a disciple is or the nature and scope of discipleship. Consequently, most Christians have to figure it out for themselves.

All baptized believers have been called and equipped to servant ministry as disciples of Jesus Christ. Our servant ministry is not to be neglected or to be taken for granted. No one else can do what God has called you to do. How you respond to your call will have either a positive or negative consequence in the kingdom of God.

BACKGROUND

Jesus, accompanied by his disciples, went back to his home, only to receive a chilly welcome from the people there. As was his custom, Jesus went to the synagogue and taught the people, who were amazed at his teaching. They were perplexed that this son of a carpenter from their small town could possess such wisdom and do such miracles. Amazingly, Jesus could not do any miracles there, except to heal a few persons, because of the people's lack of faith.

Knowing God's kingdom work must go on, Jesus went around teaching from village to village. He also sent the disciples out two by two, giving them power and authority to heal the sick and to cast out demons. As Christ's disciple, you, too, have been called to servant ministry.

A HEALING MOMENT
Read Mark 6:7-13 from the NRSV or the NKJV.

NRSV
Then he went about among the villages teaching. [7] *He called the twelve and began to send them out two by two, and gave them authority over the unclean spirits.* [8] *He ordered them to take nothing for their journey except a staff; no bread, no bag, no money in their belts;* [9] *but to wear sandals and not to put on two tunics.* [10] *He said to them, "Wherever you enter a house, stay there until you leave the place.* [11] *If any place will not welcome you and they refuse to hear you, as you leave, shake off the dust that is on your feet as a testimony against them."* [12] *So they went out and proclaimed that all should repent.* [13] *They cast out many demons, and anointed with oil many who were sick and cured them.*

NKJV
[7] *And He called the twelve to Himself, and began to send them out two by two, and gave them power over unclean spirits.* [8] *He commanded them to take nothing for the journey except a staff— no bag, no bread, no copper in their money belts—* [9] *but to wear sandals, and not to put on two tunics.* [10] *Also He said to them, "In whatever place you enter a house, stay there till you depart from that place.* [11] *And whoever will not receive you nor hear you, when you*

depart from there, shake off the dust under your feet as a testimony against them. Assuredly, I say to you, it will be more tolerable for Sodom and Gomorrah in the day of judgment than for that city!" ¹² *So they went out and preached that people should repent.* ¹³ *And they cast out many demons, and anointed with oil many who were sick, and healed them.*

DISCOVERY

1. If God's power is unlimited, why wasn't Jesus able to heal but a few sick persons?

2. There is no evidence that Jesus anointed the people he healed. Why did his disciples anoint with oil in their practice of healing?

3. If the people in his hometown did not take Jesus' ministry seriously, why would they take his disciples seriously?

4. What two things amazed the people about Jesus?

5. Why did Jesus send out the disciples in pairs of two?

6. Jesus sent out the disciples to preach and to heal from village to village. Why do you think he told them not to take any money, bread, or other personal items they might need while on the mission field?

ENCOURAGEMENT

The call to Christian service is a privilege and carries with it a great responsibility. We should never take our service to others lightly. Jesus' twelve disciples modeled for us how we are to respond to Jesus' call to discipleship. They have set very high the standard for Christian discipleship. They teach us that disciples are first and foremost students of Jesus Christ. As disciples, we are to be his closest companions. His mission is our mission. We are to love and serve those he loves. Like Jesus Christ, servant ministry is to be Spirit-empowered, Spirit-led, and Spirit-gifted. Servant ministry is always to be motivated by love, for the common good of all. The Spirit's most important gift is love that gives the other gifts their power and effectiveness. Jesus said the world would recognize his disciples by their love.

Jesus Christ gave the church two mandates to fulfill before his return, the Great Commandment and the Great Commission. Christ's church is to make disciples of all nations and to love God with her whole being. The work of God is to evangelize the world. Therefore, the spiritual gifts are to be understood as the evangelistic tools of the church. What gifts have you received to fulfill your call to servant ministry? What has hindered you from carrying out your ministry to the church?

RESPONSE

7. Although the disciples were sent out to heal the sick, what was the primary purpose of their mission?

8. What is the likelihood that you would have agreed to go out on an evangelistic mission as a disciple of Jesus without money, food, extra clothing, or prospects of a place to lodge at night?

9. Was there a specific lesson Jesus wanted his disciples to learn by sending them on an evangelistic mission without any resources?

10. Describe what you will take away from this Healing Moment that has helped to change your perspective about servant ministry.

GOING DEEPER

Have you ever been called a "Mama's boy" or "Daddy's little girl"? Rather than being a compliment, sometimes this can be a put down. The people in Jesus' hometown only saw him as the son of a carpenter. Their minds were closed to the reality that God can and does use ordinary people to do extraordinary things. They had witnessed as Jesus demonstrate God's authority and power to cast out demons and to heal people with many diseases and deformities. Although the disciples had witnessed the many miracles, they were just as blind as the people in recognizing Jesus' true identity as the Son of God, their Messiah. It is true that without the Holy Spirit's help, we see through a glass darkly.

"Looking to Jesus the pioneer and perfecter of our faith, who for the sake of the joy that was set before him endured the cross, disregarding its shame, and has taken his seat at the right hand of the throne of God" (Heb. 12:2 NRSV).

Regardless of the human failures and unbelief of his disciples, Jesus stuck with them through thick and thin. Yes, from time to time they frustrated, disappointed, and angered Jesus, but he never gave up on them or stopped believing in them. All the original twelve disciples, except the one destined to betray him, completed their mission with faithfulness and excellence.

This should give all believers hope and confidence in the service of the Lord. Jesus made this promise to his followers, "*I will never leave you or forsake you*" *(Heb. 13:5 NRSV)*. Whatever God has called you to do, you have a friend in Jesus to help you complete your work for God. For this reason, Jesus was so adamant about sending the Holy Spirit promised by the Father to equip and empower the disciples with gifts to accomplish their mission as his disciples. The Spirit will testify concerning Jesus Christ. He will assist them and us in continuing Jesus' kingdom mission.

Remember, you are not in ministry alone. The Christian life is a shared ministry in Christ. Because we participate in a shared ministry, Jesus Christ has made available to his disciples all of the resources in God's kingdom for the advancement of God's kingdom work. The body of Christ must keep in mind that God's anointing is upon the church as it was with Jesus Christ when he walked the earth. The Spirit's presence in their lives is that anointing!

The Spirit will enable and encourage the church to advance God's kingdom work. Are you ready to serve? Can God count on you?

DEVOTION
Gracious God, thank you for the gifts, abilities, talents, and graces you have bestowed on me. Give me courage and bold faith to use them to advance your kingdom and to go where you send me to serve in Christ's name. I desire to be one of your agents of change. Hear my prayer! Amen.

JOURNALING

To prepare for the next study, read Mark 6:45-56 and complete the questions for Healing Moment Eleven. Please pray for the participants and facilitators. Be prepared to have a lively discussion.

Take an inventory of the gifts, talents, abilities, and material resources you have received from the Lord. Contemplate on how God has called and equipped you to live out your discipleship in the kingdom work of Christ. Now, ask the Holy Spirit to lead and guide you as to what steps to take next. The ministry of the church is a shared ministry with Christ. Remember that Jesus promised to be with you each step you take.

HEALING FAITH, NOT MAGIC

§

CONTEMPLATION

The news about the woman who touched the hem of Jesus' garment and was miraculously healed from her bleeding problem was circulated far and wide. The people in the region believed if this woman, who had been sick for twelve years, could be healed by touching Jesus' clothes, why wouldn't that also work for them. They strongly believed God rewards faith, and they put their faith to the test.

BACKGROUND

After the miraculous feeding of the five thousand, Jesus directed his disciples to get into the boat and get away for some much needed rest. Remaining on land, Jesus went up to the mountainside to pray.

After the sun, had set, the disciples were struggling at the oars because the wind was blowing against them. From his vantage point on the mountainside, Jesus could see the disciples' boat was struggling against the strong headwinds. Concerned for their safety, Jesus left the mountainside and started walking on the lake toward their boat. Seeing him walking on water, the disciples cried out in terror and fear, thinking they were seeing a ghost.

Jesus identified himself, saying, *"Take heart, it is I; do not be afraid"* *(Mark 6:50 NRSV)*. As Jesus climbed into the boat, the winds ceased blowing, and the disciples' fears were calmed. When the people in the region saw Jesus, they gathered all their sick, carried them on mats, and laid them in the marketplaces. Wherever Jesus and the disciples went in the villages or countryside, the sick begged that they might touch his cloak. All who touched his clothes were healed.

A HEALING MOMENT
Read Mark 6:45-56 from the NRSV or the NKJV.

NRSV

45 Immediately he made his disciples get into the boat and go on ahead to the other side, to Bethsaida, while he dismissed the crowd. 46 After saying farewell to them, he went up on the mountain to pray. 47 When evening came, the boat was out on the sea, and he was alone on the land. 48 When he saw that they were straining at the oars against an adverse wind, he came towards them early in the morning, walking on the sea. He intended to pass them by. 49 But when they saw him walking on the sea, they thought it was a ghost and cried out; 50 for they all saw him and were terrified. But immediately he spoke to them and said, "Take heart, it is I; do not be afraid." 51Then he got into the boat with them, and the wind ceased. And they were utterly astounded, 52 for they did not understand about the loaves, but their hearts were hardened. 53 When they had crossed over, they came to land at Gennesaret and moored the boat. 54 When they got out of the boat, people at once recognized him, 55 and rushed about that whole region and began to bring the sick on mats to wherever they heard he was. 56 And wherever he went, into villages or cities or farms, they laid the sick in the marketplaces, and begged him that they might touch even the fringe of his cloak; and all who touched it were healed.

NKJV

⁴⁵ Immediately He made His disciples get into the boat and go before Him to the other side, to Bethsaida, while He sent the multitude away. ⁴⁶ And when He had sent them away, He departed to the mountain to pray. ⁴⁷ Now when evening came, the boat was in the middle of the sea; and He was alone on the land. ⁴⁸ Then He saw them straining at rowing, for the wind was against them. Now about the fourth watch of the night, He came to them, walking on the sea, and would have passed them by. ⁴⁹ And when they saw Him walking on the sea, they supposed it was a ghost, and cried out; ⁵⁰ for they all saw Him and were troubled. But immediately He talked with them and said to them, "Be of good cheer! It is I; do not be afraid." ⁵¹ Then He went up into the boat to them, and the wind ceased. And they were greatly amazed in themselves beyond measure, and marveled. ⁵² For they had not understood about the loaves, because their heart was hardened. ⁵³ When they had crossed over, they came to the land of Gennesaret and anchored there. ⁵⁴ And when they came out of the boat, immediately the people recognized Him, ⁵⁵ ran through that whole surrounding region, and began to carry about on beds those who were sick to wherever they heard He was. ⁵⁶ Wherever He entered, into villages, cities, or the country, they laid the sick in the marketplaces, and begged Him that they might just touch the hem of His garment. And as many as touched Him were made well.

RESPONSE

1. How would you describe the faith of those who were healed by touching Jesus' clothes?

2. Is this story of healing miracles more about magic than it is about faith? Explain.

3. By allowing the sick to touch his clothes, what does this tell us about Jesus' attitude toward human brokenness? (See Mark 5:24-34.)

4. All the people who touched Jesus' clothes were healed. How does this healing incident challenge your faith to appropriate (take possession of) your own healing?

5. Do you believe that God is with you and cares about your well-being as a servant of Christ?

6. Could one's faith initiate the creation of a miracle?

ENCOURAGEMENT

Mark underscores that the disciples had a mental and spiritual block when it came to Jesus' true identity. They seemed to be spiritually blind, incapable of interpreting the revelations of the miracles of the feeding the five thousand, Jesus' walking on water, his unique wisdom about the things of God, his power over demons, and the healing of the sick.

The disciples were not alone in their unbelief concerning the kingdom work of God. Many of us share their confusion and unbelief about who Jesus is. Paul told us that the heart of the problem is spiritual in nature, that an unspiritual person cannot understand the things of the Spirit. They are foolishness to those who are unspiritual. Paul wrote, *"Those who are unspiritual do not receive the gifts of God's Spirit, for they are foolishness to them, and they are unable to understand them because they are spiritually discerned. Those who are spiritual discern all things, and they are themselves subject to no one else's scrutiny" (1 Cor. 2:14-15 NRSV).*

So, if we want to discern the things of God, we need to have the Spirit of God dwelling within us. When, on Pentecost, the Holy Spirit was poured out on the one hundred twenty people in the Upper Room, their minds and spirits were made alive to the things of God. Only then did they understand the miracles and the things Jesus had told them. We cannot understand or do God's kingdom work without the Holy Spirit. We need the enlightenment of the Spirit to recognize Jesus' identity.

Although God's presence, power, and authority were demonstrated through Jesus, Mark concluded that no one recognized Jesus as God in human flesh. The coming of the Holy Spirit on Pentecost changed all of that for the disciples and the world.

RESPONSE

7. What motivated the people to bring their sick to be healed by Jesus?

8. Is there a connection between miracles and the kingdom of God?

9. Do you think you have a faith that could appropriate your healing miracles, as did the woman who touched the hem of Jesus' garment?

10. How might the extraordinary miracles God did through Peter's shadow (Acts 5:12-16) and Paul's handkerchiefs and aprons (Acts 19:11-12) help you better understand the healing of the woman who touched the hem of Jesus' garment (Mark 5:24-34) and the healings of the sick people in the marketplaces who touched Jesus' cloak? Explain.

11. Describe what you will take away from this Healing Moment that has helped to change your perspective on the difference between magic and expectant faith.

GOING DEEPER

Mark used a variety of miracle incidents to reveal the divine nature of Jesus. As the incarnated God in human form, he healed the sick, cast out demons, raised the dead, fed multitudes of people with five loaves of bread and two fish, walked on water, and demonstrated power over nature. Mark seemed preoccupied with a Christology of Jesus. At the same time, he also made transparently clear the disciples' struggle to connect the dots of Jesus' miracles with his divine nature.

Mark showed that people could witness the miraculous powers of God, yet not be able to rightly interpret what they see and hear because unbelief produces spiritual malaise.[1] He wanted his readers and the future disciples of Jesus Christ to realize the dangers of a negative mindset and unbelief. Mark pointed out that without faith, people live in perpetual spiritual darkness.

This same thing may also happen to believers who do not abide in Christ and in the Word of God. Paul knew that some Christian believers remain immature babies in Christ. They only crave spiritual milk and not the solid food of the Spirit—the Word of God. Their hearts become hardened, and they despise the spiritual things of God. Immature believers walk in the flesh and not in the Spirit, depending on the wisdom of this world that leads to all kinds of confusion.

The disciples could not accept Jesus' divine mission as God's suffering servant. They were looking for a messiah-king who would save them from their Roman oppressors and enemies. They were not looking for a messiah who would save them from their sins and spiritual blindness. Jesus would not allow anyone or anything to define him or his kingdom work.

DEVOTION

Loving and healing God, I do not always see things from your perspective. Sometimes my faith is weak, and I question your love and your will for my life. Like the early disciples, I don't always recognize your kindness, mercy, or compassion that comes from an all-loving and all-powerful God. Deliver me from spiritual confusion and blindness. Forgive me when I don't take the time to study your word and discover who you really are. Help me to abide in you and your word. I desire to walk in your will and your ways. Thank you for your forgiveness, mercy, and love. Thank you for hearing my prayer. In Christ Jesus' name, I pray. Amen.

JOURNALING

To prepare for the next study, read Mark 7:24-30 and complete the questions for Healing Moment Twelve. Please pray for the participants and facilitators. Be prepared to have a lively discussion.

What questions were raised, if any, by the healing incidents of those who were healed by touching Jesus' cloak? Explain.

PERSISTENT HEALING FAITH

§

CONTEMPLATION

HOW OFTEN IS YOUR FAITH tested? When you encounter disappointments, how do you respond? Too often, we give up without even putting up a good fight. We give into the temptation of believing our problems are either too big to handle or too small for God to care about. The Syrophoenician woman in this healing story teaches the importance of exercising persistent faith. Mark's gospel emphasized over and over that God is a present help in times of trouble. God is only a prayer away, and he rewards faith. The miracles of Jesus show us that God cares about every aspect of our lives. We should never forget this biblical truth!

BACKGROUND

Jesus had traveled into a region of Tyre on the Mediterranean coast, a predominantly Gentile region northwest of Galilee and about forty miles from his home base in Capernaum. He entered a house in hopes of finding seclusion and rest. A Gentile woman heard that he was in the area, learned where he was staying and went there. She fell at Jesus' feet, called him Lord, and begged him to heal her daughter who was possessed by an unclean spirit. Jesus told the woman he must first minister to the Jewish people.

The exchange he had with her is both interesting and confusing. In spite of Jesus' apparent objection to healing her daughter, she proved her faith in his ability to heal her child was just as strong as that of any Jewish mother.

A HEALING MOMENT
Read Mark 7:24-30 from the NRSV or the NKJV.

NRSV
²⁴ From there he set out and went away to the region of Tyre. He entered a house and did not want anyone to know he was there. Yet he could not escape notice, ²⁵ but a woman whose little daughter had an unclean spirit immediately heard about him, and she came and bowed down at his feet. ²⁶ Now the woman was a Gentile, of Syrophoenician origin. She begged him to cast the demon out of her daughter. ²⁷ He said to her, "Let the children be fed first, for it is not fair to take the children's food and throw it to the dogs." ²⁸ But she answered him, "Sir, even the dogs under the table eat the children's crumbs." ²⁹ Then he said to her, "For saying that, you may go—the demon has left your daughter." ³⁰ So she went home, found the child lying on the bed, and the demon gone.

NKJV
²⁴ From there He arose and went to the region of Tyre and Sidon. And He entered a house and wanted no one to know it, but He could not be hidden. ²⁵ For a woman whose young daughter had an unclean spirit heard about Him, and she came and fell at His feet. ²⁶ The woman was a Greek, a Syrophoenician by birth, and she kept asking Him to cast the demon out of her daughter. ²⁷ But Jesus said to her, "Let the children be filled first, for it is not good to take the children's bread and throw it to the little dogs." ²⁸ And she answered and said to Him, "Yes, Lord, yet even the little dogs under the table eat from the children's crumbs." ²⁹ Then He said to her, "For this saying go your way; the demon has gone out of your daughter." ³⁰ And when she had come to her house, she found the demon gone out, and her daughter lying on the bed."

DISCOVERY

1. What was the motive behind Jesus' apparent refusal to heal this
    Gentile woman's daughter?

2. What lesson does this woman teach us about persistent faith and
    resolve? (See Matt. 7:7-11.)

3. What obstacles did this mother have to overcome to get Jesus to heal her daughter?

4. Was the attitude of Jesus' disciples toward this Gentile woman racially motivated? Explain.

5. Was Jesus' statement, *"for it is not fair to take the children's bread and throw it to the dogs"* (Mk.7:27 NRSV), a put-down of the woman's daughter? Explain.

6. What impressed you most about the way this woman responded to Jesus' objection to healing her daughter?

7. What lesson do you take away from this healing incident that helps you to respond with dignity and humility toward people of another ethnic group who are in need?

ENCOURAGEMENT

The healing miracles of Jesus show us the limitless and timeless power of God. As I thought about the miracle-working power of God, it occurred to me that many miracles take place at a distance. Think about how frequently we pray for the needs of our loved ones and friends who are not present with us. In this age of technology, we text or e-mail our prayer requests. We also pray for the needs of others using this technology. We probably pray for persons by way of the telephone more than any other means. The good news is that God hears and answers those prayers, regardless of the means or distance.

It is vital that we come to understand the spiritual nature of prayer and faith, neither of which is restricted or limited by time or space. I remember watching a Pat Robertson CBN television program. He had a special guest on the program who had a prophetic ministry. Robertson asked him to look into the camera and pray for the sick. After praying, he had a prophetic message that God was healing a woman who was suffering with back pain. A woman called into the television station and gave a testimony that her back had been instantly healed through that prophecy.

At the time, this woman did not know the telecast had been prerecorded a week earlier. Regardless of the time factor, the woman's expectant faith released God's healing power, resulting in the healing of her back. This is a demonstration that God's miracle-working power transcends all boundaries, including time. Both healing stories reveal that God's power reaches beyond racial, religious, social, and ethnic boundaries. My wife, Gloria, says, "Faith is the catalyst that initiates miracles!" God rewards persistent, expectant faith! What we often forget is that God is present in human history. This is the real secret as to why miracles happen.

RESPONSE

8. Why do you think Jesus felt it necessary to test the faith of this Gentile woman before healing her daughter?

9. Does God ever act when faith is absent? Explain.

10. In what situation or circumstance has your persistent faith moved God to answer your prayers?

11. Describe what you will take away from this Healing Moment that has helped to change your perspective about the relationship between persistent faith and healing?

GOING DEEPER

As a young student pastor, some thirty-five years ago, I had been licensed to preach and appointed to my first student pastorate in a small inner-city church. I was struggling to complete my Sunday morning sermon when my youngest daughter came into the room. In her arms, she held her favorite cloth doll with plastic arms and legs. The doll was worn out. The stitching around the arms and legs was frayed and coming apart, but she loved that doll and wanted to continue to play with and enjoy the companionship of her favorite doll. With sadness in her eyes, she asked me to sew the arms and legs back to the doll's cloth body.

This was late on Saturday evening, and I felt pressure to finish the sermon before the night was gone. I said to Christina, "Daddy must finish his sermon, and I will sew up your doll later." She walked slowly out of the room with her little head bowed, disappointed and even sadder than before.

Feeling a little guilty, I commenced to putting the finishing touches to my sermon. As I looked up from my desk, Christina had come back into the room. With sad eyes, she asked me again to mend her doll. A little agitated, I told her more sternly that I could not stop working on my sermon at this time but promised I would fix her doll. Christina left the room, but in about five minutes, she was, once again, opening the door.

Guilt got the best of me, and I beckoned Christina to bring the doll to me. I got the mending kit out and began to sew one of the arms in place. As I continued to mend the doll's arms and legs, God seemed to speak to me.

God drew my attention to the torn doll, and said, "Before you knew of my love and saving grace, you were much like this doll, torn and broken. You were under the power of sin and your life was coming apart. Because I loved you, I apprehended you and saved you through the atoning sacrifice of my Son." God reminded me that I needed a complete makeover. The Lord also reminded me that he had graciously made me whole, making me a new creation in Christ, as he had intended. Using that broken and ragged doll, God spoke a personal word to me.

When I handed the doll to Christina, she gave me a big smile and a hug. We had both been touched and blessed in the love of God. Christina's persistence reminded me that God never gives up on us. God looks beyond our faults and sees our need for healing, wholeness, and salvation. This story was published in the July-August 2011 edition of *Upper Room Daily Devotional.*

That incident with my daughter, the doll, and the lesson the Lord taught me was powerful and transformative. My attitude and sermon focus were also transformed. I gained the much-needed inspiration to complete my sermon. That Sunday morning, when I stood up to preach, the sermon I had written the night before was replaced by a new sermon, birthed on Saturday night. That sermon was one of the best extemporaneous sermons I have ever preached. The congregation was touched and blessed by the sermon God helped me to preach because it demonstrated God's unconditional love for each of us.

My young daughter's persistence to get her dad to fix her doll pales in comparison to this mother's persistence in seeking deliverance for her daughter from an unclean spirit. However, both believed that their persistence would overcome all their obstacles. That is the work of faith.

Jesus recognized in this Gentile mother, a strong, persistent faith that would not be denied. The mother believed in Jesus' ability to cast out the demon from her daughter, and she would not accept defeat. Through her strong faith, she dismissed Jesus' silence and the disciples wanting to get rid of her. She envisioned her daughter delivered from that evil spirit and playing like a normal child.

In her part of the world, many persons were known as miracle workers. Not wanting to be labeled as just a miracle worker, Jesus tested the woman's faith to see if she thought of him in this way.[1] Jesus told the Gentile woman it was not right to take the children's bread and throw it to dogs. The woman did not take Jesus' words as an insult. She further let Jesus know she understood divine grace, knowing that she did not have to deserve grace to receive it and realizing that even the dogs under the children's tables eat the crumbs that fall to the floor.

Her persistent faith moved Jesus to grant her petition, telling her to go home, her daughter was healed. In faith, the mother took Jesus at his word, went home, and found her daughter lying on a bed, healed. The demon was gone. This is the first healing miracle in Mark's gospel that Jesus performed from a distance.

The woman's expectant and persistent faith was rewarded in the healing of her daughter. She became his first test case, revealing that Gentiles were open and receptive to his message of healing, wholeness, and salvation. Mark showed that when the gospel of the kingdom is proclaimed in the spirit and compassion of Jesus Christ and the love and power of God, it becomes a message of good news for Jews and Gentiles alike. This became the primary mission of the church, to proclaim the gospel of salvation, first to the Jews and, through them to all nations. Healing is to be a central part of proclaiming the gospel of salvation. Someone has said, "Teaching explains the gospel, preaching proclaims the gospel, but healing makes real the gospel."

DEVOTION
Almighty God, your love, mercy, and grace transcend all boundaries. Thank you that I am included. You love all peoples, regardless of their race, religion, social, and economic status. Through your Son, Jesus Christ, you have proven your love, that while we were still sinners, Jesus Christ died for the sins of the whole world. Your love is amazing! Your love has set us free. Help me to live in your love and to share that love with everyone I meet. In Christ's name, I pray. Amen.

JOURNALING
To prepare for the next study, read Mark 7:31-37 and complete the questions for Healing Moment Thirteen. Please pray for the participants and facilitators. Be prepared to have a lively discussion.

Think back and recall how you first heard the good news of salvation. How did you first respond to the message of salvation? What has changed since you were saved?

GOD'S HEALING GRACE INCLUDES EVERYONE

§

CONTEMPLATION

Most Christians have heard the statement, "God is not a respecter of persons" (Acts 10:34-35; 2 Peter 3:9; 1 Tim. 2:4 KJV). God does not show favoritism. God also does not want the followers of Christ to show favoritism (James 2:9). Jesus and the apostle Paul reminded us that "all have sinned and fall short of the glory of God" (Rom. 3:23). In Jesus Christ, both Jews and Gentiles alike stand before God on a level playing field and need God's healing and saving grace. Jesus' atoning death on the cross is God's equalizer, the ultimate expression of God's unconditional love. Through his atoning death, Jesus has opened the way for everyone to experience God's healing, wholeness, and salvation.

BACKGROUND

Mark records three miracles Jesus performed as he ministered in a region of the Gentiles. As Jesus and his disciples traveled from Tyre through Sidon toward the Sea of Galilee, in the region of the Decapolis, he encountered a deaf man with a speech impediment. The man's friends brought him to Jesus, begging him to heal their friend. This healing is unique to Mark's gospel. It is significant because Jesus had just taught the disciples there is no difference between Jews and Gentiles, for all are sinners and need a savior.[1]

This miracle is unique in several ways. The man brought to Jesus was deaf and could not communicate because of his speech impediment. Jesus took the man away from the people to minister to him in private. He personalized his healing methods to bring about the best results. Because there could be no communication between Jesus and the man, Jesus used touch as a means of communication. He put his fingers into the man's ears, then he spat and touched the man's tongue. Looking up to the heaven, he sighed and said, "Ephphatha!" Mark translated this Aramaic word, which means "be opened," for his Roman readers. Mark wanted the people to know that this was an actual word and not some kind of ritual or incantation used by the miracle workers of Jesus' day.

Jesus used touch, a compassionate prayer, spit, a private ministry, and the faith of the man to loosen his tongue and to open his ears. The man received a double blessing of God's healing grace, allowing him to hear perfectly and speak plainly. This miracle was too amazing for the people to keep it to themselves, as Jesus had ordered them to do. They spread the news about the miracle far and wide, amazing the people.

A HEALING MOMENT
Read Mark 7:31-37 from the NRSV or the NKJV.

NRSV
[31] *Then he returned from the region of Tyre, and went by way of Sidon towards the Sea of Galilee, in the region of the Decapolis.* [32] *They brought to him a deaf man who had an impediment in his speech; and they begged him to lay his hand on him.* [33] *He took him aside in private, away from the crowd, and put his fingers into his ears, and he spat and touched his tongue.* [34] *Then looking up to heaven, he*

sighed and said to him, "Ephphatha," that is, "Be opened." ³⁵And immediately his ears were opened, his tongue was released, and he spoke plainly. ³⁶Then Jesus ordered them to tell no one; but the more he ordered them, the more zealously they proclaimed it. ³⁷ They were astounded beyond measure, saying, "He has done everything well; he even makes the deaf to hear and the mute to speak."

NKJV

³¹Again, departing from the region of Tyre and Sidon, He came through the midst of the region of Decapolis to the Sea of Galilee. ³²Then they brought to Him one who was deaf and had an impediment in his speech, and they begged Him to put His hand on him. ³³And He took him aside from the multitude, and put His fingers in his ears, and He spat and touched his tongue. ³⁴Then, looking up to heaven, He sighed, and said to him, "Ephphatha," that is, "Be opened." ³⁵ Immediately his ears were opened, and the impediment of his tongue was loosed, and he spoke plainly. ³⁶Then He commanded them that they should tell no one; but the more He commanded them, the more widely they proclaimed it. ³⁷And they were astonished beyond measure, saying, "He has done all things well. He makes both the deaf to hear and the mute to speak."

DISCOVERY

1. Do you believe your physical and spiritual conditions matter to God? Explain why or why not.

2. What do you suppose Jesus prayed about as he sighed, looking up to heaven?

3. What surprised you most about the healing of the deaf and mute man?

4. What did Jesus teach you about healing that both encouraged and inspired a desire within you to pray for the sick and suffering?

5. What would the church and world look and feel like if the practice of healing were limited only to a certain group of people?

6. You may not have the gift of healing, but what gifts do you have to share in Jesus' ministry of compassion to people who are suffering?

ENCOURAGEMENT

The gospel of Jesus Christ is inclusive. People are not excluded because of their ethnic background or religious affiliation, or whether they are rich or poor, slave or free. God's salvation is free but not cheap. Jesus accepted death on a cross to purchase our healing, wholeness, and salvation.

Jesus invites us to come to God as we are. His death opened the way to all healing. We must come to God in faith, trusting in his mercy, forgiveness, and grace. You don't have to understand grace to receive it. God's love is available to all, but you must choose to receive it. God wants everyone to be a whole person.

God heard Jesus' compassionate sigh; he saw his concern for the deaf and mute man. God hears your prayers as well. The prayer for healing will always be answered, either in this life or in the life to come. It will come! Keep believing it is the goodness of God. And when you receive it, tell others about the goodness of God.

RESPONSE

7. Jesus and his disciples were tired to the bone, yet Jesus reached out to this deaf and mute man. What excuses do you make for not reaching out to those around you who are hurting?

8. In what ways have you allowed the love of money and material things to blind you to the needs of people around you?

9. How is God calling you to share in Christ's ministry to the hurting and suffering people in your church and community?

10. As you look at the hurting and suffering people in your church community, what gift or gifts would you ask God for to minister to those needs?

GOING DEEPER

The way Jesus healed this man tells us how deeply he cares about the health and well-being of people. He put the well-being of others above his own needs. Jesus' servant heart was always on display. When he told his disciples, they were to model ministry after him; he meant they were to demonstrate his compassion as well as his servant's heart (John 14:12).

Having served the church for over thirty-five years, I know from personal experience how difficult and challenging ministry can be. There are no shortcuts. Like Jesus, we are to do ministry through our dependence on God. On several occasions, Jesus said he did nothing on his own, and he did only what he saw the Father doing. This is how we are to do ministry as well. We must resist the temptation of doing ministry in our own way and our own strength. We are likewise to resist the temptation of carrying out ministry as a lone ranger. Both temptations are doomed to failure.

Jesus discovered early on that a team ministry is more productive and rewarding. In ministry, we need the support, help, and encouragement of others. Christian ministry is a shared ministry. Observing the healing miracles, we also learn from Jesus that each ministry opportunity requires different skills and methods to achieve the best outcome. Observing Jesus in ministry reveals that servant ministry is Spirit-led and Spirit-empowered, tempered with compassion and *agape* love.

By touching the man, Jesus made a personal connection between the sick man and himself, giving him confidence and assurance of his presence, as well as his power to heal him. Jesus teaches that ministry is as much about presence as it is power. The sequence of Jesus' touch, prayer, and presence indicated to the man that he was to expect to be healed from the one who stood in front of him.[2] Jesus fully believed that God's healing power was available to him to liberate the man from his infirmities. The man's ears were opened, his tongue was loosed, and the amazed Gentiles glorified

God. True kingdom ministry should liberate the sick as well as those who witnessed the miracle. The people witnessed what can happen in their lives. As witnesses of God's grace, presence, and power, the role of the church is to bring the sick and suffering to God's healing Messiah— Jesus Christ.

DEVOTION

Loving God, I am thankful that, in Christ, you have made your presence, grace, and healing power available to your hurting and suffering people. The prophet Isaiah foretold the coming of the healing-Christ. His mission is to save your people. The sick and suffering are promised that they will be strengthened and healed. The good news of your salvation is amazing and gives me hope. The Messiah of God will open the ears of the deaf, cause the lame to leap for joy, and loosen the tongue to cause the speechless to sing your praises (Isa. 35ff). Open my eyes to see those in need around me. Loosen my tongue to speak for those who have no voice. Give me a heart of compassion like your Son, Jesus Christ. Show me where I can make a difference right where I live and serve. Amen.

JOURNALING

To prepare for the next study, read Mark 8:22-26 and complete the questions for Healing Moment Fourteen. Please pray for the participants and facilitators. Be prepared to have a lively discussion.

Read Isaiah 35:5-10 in light of the healing of the deaf and mute man in Mark 7:31-37. How does this Old Testament passage of the promise of restoration and healing help you to look to God for your healing?

A MIRACLE THAT REQUIRED
TWO ATTEMPTS

§

CONTEMPLATION

Wilson Pickett, a pioneer soul singer, wrote the 1966 hit song, "Ninety-Nine and One-Half Won't Do." Some in the Christian community put a spiritual twist on Wilson's song, giving the song a more Christian subtext. As we seek to live a Christian life—or seek healing or desire to walk before God in faithfulness—ninety-nine and one-half won't do. Christ calls believers to go all the way with God without compromise.

A scriptural example of this is when Jesus laid his hand on the blind man, and he was only partially healed. His vision was still blurred, and he could not see at a distance. He saw men looking like trees. Jesus was, in fact, saying, "Ninety-nine and one-half won't do." This was the first time Jesus has to pray twice to heal anyone. Because of the partial healing of the blind man, Jesus laid his hand on his eyes a second time.

BACKGROUND

The ministry of Jesus and his disciples had taken them to Bethsaida, on the north shore of the Sea of Galilee. During this final miraculous event of Jesus' Galilean ministry, some people brought to him a blind man and begged Jesus to heal him. Jesus' response seems to suggest he discerned a lack of faith.

Jesus decided to heal the blind man outside of the village. His discernment seemed to be confirmed because he had difficulty healing the blind man. When the man received his sight, Jesus instructed him to go home, not even to go back into the village. The people sang praises to Jesus Christ who had done all things well, causing the deaf to hear, the mute to speak, and the blind to see.

A HEALING MOMENT
Read Mark 8:22-26 from the NRSV or the NKJV.

NRSV
22 They came to Bethsaida. Some people brought a blind man to him and begged him to touch him. 23 He took the blind man by the hand and led him out of the village; and when he had put saliva on his eyes and laid his hands on him, he asked him, "Can you see anything?" 24 And the man looked up and said, "I can see people, but they look like trees, walking." 25 Then Jesus laid his hands on his eyes again; and he looked intently and his sight was restored, and he saw everything clearly. 26 Then he sent him away to his home, saying, "Do not even go into the village."

NKJV
22 Then He came to Bethsaida; and they brought a blind man to Him, and begged Him to touch him. 23 So He took the blind man by the hand and led him out of the town. And when He had spit on his eyes and put His hands on him, He asked him if he saw anything. 24 And he looked up and said, "I see men like trees, walking." 25 Then He put His hands on his eyes again and made him look up. And he was restored and saw everyone clearly. 26 Then He sent him away to his house, saying, "Neither go into the town, nor tell anyone in the town."

RESPONSE

1. What made the healing of the blind man an unusual healing event?

2. How are the healings of the deaf man (Mark 7:31-37) and the blind man (Mark 8:22-26) both weird and wonderful at the same time?

3. Did Mark intend a connection between the apparent spiritual blindness of the disciples and the two men healed by Jesus of their blindness? (See Mark 8:22-26; 10:46-52.)

4. List several things that make this healing story different from all the others Jesus performed (Mark 8:22-26).

5. Is there evidence that this man was not born blind?

6. Considering that Jesus had to lay his hands on the blind man's eyes a second time before he was completely healed, what should the church learn from this healing story?

7. Although the healing of the blind man was a two-step and
   gradual process, can it still be considered a miracle?

ENCOURAGEMENT

This healing miracle seems strange and unconventional. It is the
first miracle that occurred gradually and not instantly. During the
time of Jesus, it was not uncommon to put spit on the man's eyes.[2]
Perhaps putting saliva on his eyes and touching his eyes were done
to initiate a response of his other senses and to activate his faith.[3]
The healings performed by Jesus were personal and individual.

Although I have had the privilege of praying for hundreds,
if not thousands, of people, very few deaf and blind people have
asked for healing. Perhaps this is because many believe that these
infirmities are more difficult to heal.

Blind Bartimaeus and the other blind persons Jesus healed
would strongly disagree with this notion. Bartimaeus believed Jesus
had the power to heal him.

RESPONSE

8. Why do you think Jesus isolated himself from the people in the healing of this blind man?

9. The gospels recorded Jesus' healing at least seven persons who were blind. List the different methods he used to heal each of them.

10. Why do you think Jesus used different methods to heal the blind and people in general?

GOING DEEPER

You may recall the story of Herod putting John the Baptist in prison at his wife's wishes because John did not approve of Herod marrying his brother's wife. While in prison, John struggled in his faith concerning whether Jesus was indeed the Christ who was to come. Hearing of the miraculous things Jesus was doing, John sent some of his disciples to ask Jesus if he was truly the Christ or were they to wait for another. Jesus told John's disciples, *"Go and tell John what you hear and see: the blind receives their sight, the lame walk, the lepers are cleansed, the deaf hear, the dead are raised, and the poor have good news brought to them. And blessed is anyone who takes no offense at me"* (Matt. 11:4a-6 NRSV).

The fact that Jesus was performing various miracles—giving sight to the blind, causing the lame to walk, cleansing lepers, making the deaf to hear, and even raising the dead—should have caused all who witnessed these awesome deeds to confess their sins and call out to God, "What must I do to be saved?" Miracles are powerful signs that God wants everyone to be well and whole. Jesus came to bring forgiveness, healing, and salvation to the world, restoring God's good creation.

In Jesus Christ, God has defeated our enemies, those within us and those outside of us. Jesus' coming is a sign that God has ushered in a kingdom of grace, mercy, forgiveness, healing, and salvation. Jesus said this much to John the Baptist. We should believe it and rejoice that our salvation is closer than we think.

Can you see that healing replaced the curse of God that occurred in the Fall? God in Christ looks beyond our faults and sees our needs. Are you able to see that our real enemy, Satan, is defeated by Jesus' death on the cross? Jesus Christ has come full of grace and truth. The truth is that God now offers us grace not only to be forgiven and saved but also offers us grace to live victorious lives, to live in righteousness and holiness. This is what Satan is working so feverishly to keep us from, so he inflicts us with sickness and disease to cause us to distrust the goodness of God. If Satan can inflict us physically, mentally (emotionally), spiritually, and relationally, he distorts God's image in us. By distorting God's image in us, we will begin to hate ourselves and others.

Jesus told John the Baptist to see in the miraculous healings the restoration of His image as being restored in his creation. The healing miracles of Jesus are a sign of the restoration of God's good creation, reversing the effects and consequences of the Fall. Christ Jesus brings both restoration and liberation. Both are signs of the coming kingdom rule and reign of God.

Jesus made his mission and ministry of the kingdom of God a mandate for the church, the body of Christ. He gave his power and authority to the church to heal the sick, cleanse the leper, cast out demons, and raise the dead (Matt. 10:1-2, 7-8; Mark 3:16- 19; 6:8-11; Luke 9:1-2; 10:4-12; 10:19-22). The church is to continue Jesus' threefold ministry of teaching, preaching, and healing. The church is a spiritual hospital, according to the apostle James. James instructs the sick to call on the elders of the church to anoint and pray for their healing.

Healing is a sign to the world that God's kingdom reign has come in the person of the Healing Messiah. Finally, the two healing miracles involving blind men have several things in common in wording, and each story seems to point to Isaiah 35:5-6. In each incident, the people bring the person needing healing to Jesus. Discerning a lack of faith in both accounts, Jesus heals the two persons away from the community.

Mark is the only gospel that records Jesus putting saliva on the eyes of the blind persons before healing them (7:33; 8:22) as part of the two-step healing process of the blind and mute.[4] All of Jesus' healing miracles reveal that nothing is impossible to God. God desires wholeness for all people because healing and salvation are inseparable.

DEVOTION

God of creation, thank you that I am wonderfully and fearfully made (Ps. 139). Thank you for my eyesight to see your beautiful creation and all the things your hands have made. I am looking forward to beholding the awesome beauty of heaven. The Bible tells me that in heaven, the streets are paved with gold. There are many gates made of pearls. Heaven is filled with the light of your presence and the glory of Christ sitting at Your right hand. What a sight to behold. I look forward to making heaven my home with all the saints of God. In Jesus' name, amen.

JOURNALING

To prepare for the next study, read Mark 9:14-29 and complete the questions for Healing Moment Fifteen. Please pray for the participants and facilitators. Be prepared to have a lively discussion.

Describe how God may be calling you to use your eyesight in your service to others.

PRAYER, NOT HUMAN POWER, OVERCOMES DEMONS

§

CONTEMPLATION

Our plans and expectations are often disrupted by disappointments and regrets. When we put our faith and hopes in people and things, even our best plans can go awry. Andre Crouch wrote a much-loved song titled "Jesus Is the Answer." The chorus of the song says, *"Jesus is the answer for the world today."*

The father of a demon-possessed boy had hope and conviction that Jesus would deliver his son from tormenting demon. He believed this about Jesus' ability to heal his son. The truth is, Jesus was the answer for the healing of this boy, he is our answer today, and he will be the answer for future generations.

BACKGROUND

Peter, James, and John went with Jesus up a high mountain. When they arrived, they were surprised that Moses and Elijah met with Jesus. They witnessed the transfiguration of Jesus. Then a cloud overshadowed them, and from the cloud, they heard the voice of God, saying: *"This is my Son, the Beloved; listen to him!" (Mark 9:7 NRSV).* As they traveled down the mountain where the other disciples waited,

Jesus ordered them not to tell anyone about what they had seen until after the Son of Man had been raised from the dead. This they did.

When they rejoined the other disciples, they saw a large crowd around them. Some scribes were arguing with them. When the people saw Jesus, they were immediately overwhelmed with awe and ran to greet him. Jesus asked the scribes what they were arguing about. From the crowd, the father explained: "*Teacher, I brought you my son; he has a spirit that makes him unable to speak; and whenever it seizes him, it dashes him down; and he foams and grinds his teeth and becomes rigid; and I asked your disciples to cast it out, but they could not do so*" (Mark 9:17-18 NRSV).

Jesus showed his displeasure toward the nine disciples who had failed in casting out the demon. In a strong tone, Jesus told them they should have been able to cast the demons out. Jesus rebuked the unclean spirits to prove God's absolute power over demons. This dismayed the scribes and bewildered and discouraged his disciples, but it brought joy to the father. Jesus strongly rebuked the unclean spirit for keeping this boy from speaking and hearing and commanded it to come out and never enter him again. The boy was also suffering from a form of epilepsy.[1]

The unclean spirit, wanting to get in its final licks, showed some defiance. As it left, it shook the boy violently, causing him to fall to the ground as if he were dead. Jesus knew that all the demon's tactics were done in defiance, though the demon knew it had been defeated by God's power, working in Jesus. Jesus lifted the boy to his feet, showing his authority and victory over the unclean spirit. Jesus then commanded the unclean spirit never to trouble the boy again. Jesus proved God's absolute power over demons by commanding the evil spirit to leave the boy.

In private, the disciples asked Jesus why they could not cast the demon out. Jesus explained that prayer is essential to overpowering Satan and his demonic realm. Human power is no substitute for prayer. Demons do not respond to human power, but they are subject to believers who are people of prayer. Prayer and the Word of God are the only things that will defeat Satan and his demons, every time and in every situation. Jesus made it clear that prayer is the source that releases divine power to defeat Satan and his demonic realm.

A HEALING MOMENT
Read Mark 9:14-29 from the NRSV or the NKJV.

NRSV

14 When they came to the disciples, they saw a great crowd around them, and some scribes arguing with them. 15 When the whole crowd saw him, they were immediately overcome with awe, and they ran forward to greet him. 16 He asked them, "What are you arguing about with them?" 17 Someone from the crowd answered him, "Teacher, I brought you my son; he has a spirit that makes him unable to speak; 18 and whenever it seizes him, it dashes him down; and he foams and grinds his teeth and becomes rigid; and I asked your disciples to cast it out, but they could not do so." 19 He answered them, "You faithless generation, how much longer must I be among you? How much longer must I put up with you? Bring him to me." 20 And they brought the boy to him. When the spirit saw him, immediately it convulsed the boy, and he fell on the ground and rolled about, foaming at the mouth. 21 Jesus asked the father, "How long has this been happening to him?" And he said, "From childhood. 22 It has often cast him into the fire and into the water, to destroy him; but if you are able to do anything, have pity on us and help us." 23 Jesus said to him, "If you are able!—All things can be done for the one who believes." 24 Immediately the father of the child cried out, "I believe; help my unbelief!" 25 When Jesus saw that a crowd came running together, he rebuked the unclean spirit, saying to it, "You spirit that keeps this boy from speaking and hearing, I command you, come out of him, and never enter him again!" 26 After crying out and convulsing him terribly, it came out, and the boy was like a corpse, so that most of them said, "He is dead." 27 But Jesus took him by the hand and lifted him up, and he was able to stand. 28 When he had entered the house, his disciples asked him privately, "Why could we not cast it out?" 29 He said to them, "This kind can come out only through prayer."

NKJV

¹⁴ And when He came to the disciples, He saw a great multitude around them, and scribes disputing with them. ¹⁵ Immediately, when they saw Him, all the people were greatly amazed, and running to Him, greeted Him. ¹⁶ And He asked the scribes, "What are you discussing with them?"

¹⁷ Then one of the crowd answered and said, "Teacher, I brought You my son, who has a mute spirit. ¹⁸ And wherever it seizes him, it throws him down; he foams at the mouth, gnashes his teeth, and becomes rigid. So, I spoke to Your disciples, that they should cast it out, but they could not."

¹⁹ He answered him and said, "O faithless generation, how long shall I be with you? How long shall I bear with you? Bring him to Me." ²⁰ Then they brought him to Him. And when he saw Him, immediately the spirit convulsed him, and he fell on the ground and wallowed, foaming at the mouth.

²¹ So He asked his father, "How long has this been happening to him?"

And he said, "From childhood. ²² And often he has thrown him both into the fire and into the water to destroy him. But if You can do anything, have compassion on us and help us."

²³ Jesus said to him, "If you can believe, all things are possible to him who believes. ²⁴ Immediately the father of the child cried out and said with tears, "Lord, I believe; help my unbelief!"

²⁵ When Jesus saw that the people came running together, He rebuked the unclean spirit, saying to it: "Deaf and dumb spirit, I command you, come out of him and enter him no more!" ²⁶ Then the spirit cried out, convulsed him greatly, and came out of him. And he became as one dead, so that many said, "He is dead." ²⁷ But Jesus took him by the hand and lifted him up, and he arose.

²⁸ And when He had come into the house, His disciples asked Him privately, "Why could we not cast it out?" ²⁹ So He said to them, "This kind can come out by nothing but prayer and fasting."

DISCOVERY

1. What caused Jesus to be so exasperated with his disciples concerning this healing incident?

2. The disciples had successfully cast out demons previously. Why were they unable to cast out this unclean spirit from the boy?

3. Did the disciples' inability to cast out the demon from the boy shake the father's confidence in Jesus' ability to heal his son?

4. Are you letting God use the gifts He has given you to liberate your brothers and sisters from the work of evil spirits? If so, in what ways?

5. Why is prayer necessary in casting out evil spirits?

6. Is there ever a time when human power is a substitute for prayer in casting out an evil spirit? Explain.

7. Describe a situation when you failed to accomplish a spiritual task because you had not spent quality time with God in prayer. What lesson did you learn from that experience?

ENCOURAGEMENT

Mark's gospel clearly emphasized the continuous struggle and confrontation between Satan and Jesus. He consistently showed that, although Satan is a formidable foe in the world, he is also a defeated foe. Jesus defeated him on the cross and rendered him powerless against the redeemed of God. When God raised Jesus from the dead, and he ascended to the right hand of God, Satan's eternal fate was sealed. God has given to the resurrected Christ all power and authority. Jesus Christ has conferred his power and authority over Satan to the church. (See Luke 10:17-20.) The resurrected Christ now lives and works in, and through the church, the body of Christ, and the gates of hell shall not prevail against Christ's church (Matt. 16:17-19).

Satan still wields power over those in the world who are lost and living in sin. Because of sin, the world is still under his evil influence. He is still going around *"like a roaring lion, seeking whom he may devour"* (1 Peter 5:8, NKJV). He is still oppressing people, trying to frustrate the kingdom work of God and being a thorn in the church's side.

John the Revelator pointed out that Satan has turned his wrath against people because he knows that his time is short (Rev. 12:12). This is why the demons raised these questions to Jesus Christ: *"What have you to do with us, Jesus of Nazareth? Have you come to destroy us?" (Mark 1:24, 34; 3:11; 5:7-8 NRSV).* The demonic realm knows who Jesus is, who sent him, and why he has come. What they don't know is when God will ultimately destroy them. So, they are working overtime to accomplish as much destruction and to frustrate God's kingdom work as they can. We only need to observe the evil in our world. Satan uses groups like Isis and other hate groups to do his evil will in the world, spreading horrific crimes against human beings who do not subscribe to their religious ideology and social system of belief. It does not stop there, but includes systemic methods of oppression, promoting poverty, poor education, mass incarcerations, lack of decent housing and health care, limited economic opportunities, and more. All forms of oppression are rooted in the evil of whom Satan is behind.

The apostle Paul reminds us that we wrestle not with flesh and blood— human beings. The good news is that those who have died in Christ are motivated by love, and seek to create the beloved community that promotes justice and righteousness toward all people. Having died in Christ, we no longer live for ourselves. We are Christ's ambassadors, seeking to reconcile others to Christ. (See 2 Cor. 5:17-20.)

Jesus gave the church power and authority over the works of Satan. This same power frees us to love God and neighbor, fulfilling the Great Commandment. The Bible calls this the Spirit-filled life. The Holy Spirit makes the resurrected Christ's presence and power available to the redeemed of the Lord, the priesthood of all believers. When the church moves in love, unity, and purpose, Christ's presence, power, and authority will be manifested through his body to defeat Satan's evil influence in the world.

RESPONSE

8. List several ways prayer affects one's faith.

9. How did the verbal exchange between Jesus and the father strengthen the father's faith?

10. Previously, the disciples had cast out demons. (See Mark 6:13.) What do Matthew and Luke give as the reason why the disciples were unable to cast out the evil spirits in the boy? (See Matt. 17:14- 19; Luke 9:37-45.)

11. Read the following passages of scripture: Mark 1:23-27; 5:1-20; 9:14-29). What patterns of demonic activity did Mark want his readers to pay attention to?

12. In the deliverance ministry of the church, faith and prayer are spiritual twins necessary to release God's power over demons. Explain.

GOING DEEPER

The gospel of Mark recorded four exorcisms performed by Jesus. Using the healing miracle of the boy with the evil spirit, Mark captured the significance of all the exorcisms and emphasized their importance to the overall mission and ministry of Jesus and in the life and ministry of his future church. It is important to recall that exorcism not only defines a central component of Jesus' messianic mission but is essential to our understanding of God's kingdom work of redemption. Jesus came to set the captives free. Exorcism and healing represent the work of the kingdom of God and are not to be treated as independent events. Therefore Jesus constantly silenced the demons from making him known and why he also told those he healed not to tell anyone he had healed them. Jesus told the three disciples who witnessed his transfiguration not to tell anyone about it until after his death and resurrection. Healing and exorcism are to be interpreted within the context of the kingdom reign of God. Jesus did not want just to be known as a healer. He was not only God's Healing Messiah, but was also the redeeming Christ, who would suffer and die on a cross for the sins of Israel and the world. Mark did not want his readers to lose sight of Jesus' redemptive purpose as Israel's Messiah. His messianic mission ushered in God's kingdom reign or rule—as a healer and —Savior of the world.

Healing, health, wholeness, deliverance, and salvation are works of God's kingdom. To separate them from God's kingdom work is to misunderstand the gospel of the kingdom. Therefore, the scripture reveals that healing is in the atonement.

Since the sin of Adam, humankind lived under God's curse. Now, grace has come through the one man, Jesus Christ. Grace is God's unmerited favor shown to those who put their trust in God's salvation, offered through the atoning death of Jesus Christ on the tree. Jesus became our curse. Paul says it this way: "Christ purchased our freedom [redeeming us] from the curse (doom) of the Law [and its condemnation] by [Himself] becoming a curse for us, for it is written [in the Scriptures], Cursed is everyone who hangs on a tree (is crucified)" (Gal. 3:13 AMP).

Although Satan used the disobedience of Adam and Eve to introduce sin, human brokenness, and death into God's good creation, God was still in control. God's plan for creation would ultimately succeed. God's divine initiative through Jesus Christ, his Son, would bring about the restoration of God's good creation. Healing is a sign of that restoration. Healing and salvation are the two sides of the same coin—divine grace. God sent his Son Jesus Christ to become the sacrificial lamb to take away the sin of the world that spread from Adam to the whole world.

This brings us back to the disciples' misunderstanding of the authority given to them by Jesus. Mark pointed out that the disciples' failure to cast out the demon in the boy resulted from several miscalculations. First, they miscalculated the strength and destructive nature of the evil spirit that had this boy in its grip. Second, they miscalculated the weakness of human power against the cunningness, strength, and resolve of demons to keep their victims bound and under their control. Third, the disciples failed to realize the important role that prayer plays in building and strengthening one's faith. Demons know that human power is no match with their supernatural power. They will always challenge weak and immature faith.

Fourth, the disciples lacked an understanding of their spiritual dependence on the power and authority of God through Jesus Christ. Their failure to cast out the evil spirit was a direct reflection of Jesus because they represented his spiritual and divine authority over demons, and their evil influence in the world. Their ministry was an extension of Jesus' ministry. They failed to understand this fact. Jesus often made it clear to them that he did nothing on his own. Jesus said that he only did his Father's will. He further told the Pharisees that he cast out demons by the power of the Spirit of God. The disciples failed to realize that only by the Spirit of God could they cast out demons and not by their human attributes. This is what made Jesus so upset and disappointed that they did not have this understanding of who they were in him—God's kingdom work. Jesus said, *"O unbelieving generation ... how long shall I stay with you?"* (Mark 9:19 NIV). In other words, Jesus was saying his disciples should have been able to heal the boy by casting out the evil spirit. The disciples had failed to stand in Jesus' place and to demonstrate his power. They were trusting in themselves rather than in God.[1] The evil spirits knew this and resisted their efforts, discounting their power to help the boy. Demons will obey Jesus' followers only when they recognize the Spirit of Jesus Christ (in them) and their dependence on him. Although we are gifted with God's charismata (gifts) and authority, we don't make them work. We must ask in prayer and in faith that God activate his gifts and power in and through us. The disciples forgot this important spiritual principle.[2]

Finally, God's original plan was to use the disciples to heal this father's boy. God had designed this healing moment as their faith building opportunity. We know that God wanted the boy to be healed because Jesus healed him. How often do we miss the opportunity to be a part of what God is doing? How many times have we had the wrong mindset or not been prepared spiritually to be used by God to make a difference in the lives of others? We will continue to miss those divine moments when we don't spend quality time with God in prayer and studying of His Word. Both are essential for faith development and Christian service.

DEVOTION

Gracious and merciful God, I often take for granted that Jesus had to die a horrific death on the cross to ultimately defeat Satan on my behalf and for the world. Help me to trust you fully and not in myself as I do your kingdom work. Thank you for the Holy Spirit working in and through me to bring healing and deliverance to those who are oppressed by the devil. Help me to bring you praise, glory, and honor in all that I do in Christ's name. Amen.

JOURNALING

To prepare for the next study, read Mark 10:46-52 and complete the questions for Healing Moment Sixteen. Please pray for the participants and facilitators. Be prepared to have a lively discussion.

Dr. William L. Lane, in his *Commentary on the Gospel of Mark,* gives us valuable insight to the kind of faith that is required to experience the miracle of deliverance: *"When faith confronts the demonic, God's omnipotence is its sole assurance, and God's sovereignty is the only restriction. This is the faith which experiences the miracle of deliverance."*[3]

Write down the insight you have gained from Dr. Lane's statement concerning faith and deliverance.

YOUR FAITH HAS MADE YOU WELL

§

CONTEMPLATION

The healing of blind Bartimaeus is the last healing account recorded in Mark's gospel. First, it is significant because Bartimaeus was the first recipient of Jesus' healing whom Mark named. Second, it is noteworthy for being the only healing miracle of a blind person whom Jesus neither touched nor prayed for. He simply declared, *"Go, your faith has made you well"(Mark 10:52a NRSV).*

Third, Mark emphasized the importance of personal faith in the healing process. According to Mark, faith is the catalyst that releases God's power to heal. Mark affirmed that God rewards expectant and persistent faith. Bartimaeus possessed that kind of faith. God does not validate unbelief or doubt. James affirmed this spiritual principle (James 1:6-8). Fourth, Mark stressed over and over that human wholeness, or well-being is central in mind and will of God for His creation.

BACKGROUND

The healing of Bartimaeus was a defining moment in the mission of Jesus, concluding his Galilean ministry. Jesus' focus was now on Jerusalem and the cross. As he and his disciples were leaving Jericho, he encountered a beggar named Bartimaeus, sitting by the roadside begging for money. Hearing the commotion of the people traveling by the blind man asked what was going on. Someone from the crowd told him that Jesus was passing by. Bartimaeus cried out, *"Son of David, have mercy on me" (Mk. 10:48 NRSV!"* Many in the crowd tried to silence him, but the more they tried, the more he cried out to Jesus. His cries stopped Jesus in his tracks, and he told the people to call to him.

Bartimaeus immediately threw off his outer garment and made his way to Jesus. Jesus asked him, *"What do you want me to do for you (MK. 10:50 NRSV)?"* Bartimaeus replied, *"My teacher, let me see again."* Without touching him or saying a prayer for his healing, Jesus commended him for his faith and said, *"Go; your faith has made you well" Mk.:52 NRSV).*Immediately, he regained his sight and followed Jesus on the way.

What is extraordinary about the healing of Bartimaeus is that there seems to be an air of expectancy and excitement in Jesus. Perhaps hearing Bartimaeus calling him by his messianic title, Son of David (used only in the synoptic gospels), may have caused Jesus to reflect on his mission as the savior of his Jewish people and the world. Jesus made many claims that he is the messianic hope of Israel.

Even though the ordeal of the cross loomed in Jesus' immediate future, he took the time to heal a blind man sitting by the road. This healing was a significant transition in Jesus' life and ministry and would be such in the life of his disciples. His earthly kingdom work was coming to its divine end, while the disciples' ministry was just beginning. Jesus' focus now shifted to Jerusalem and the cross. He went to the Jewish feast to embrace his messianic vocation.[1] This was an indication that his mission was on the right course. The road leading to the cross opened a path to God's redemption work to bring salvation to Israel and the world.

A HEALING MOMENT
Read Mark 10:46-52 from the NRSV or the NKJV.

NRSV

⁴⁶ They came to Jericho. As he and his disciples and a large crowd were leaving Jericho, Bartimaeus son of Timaeus, a blind beggar, was sitting by the roadside. ⁴⁷ When he heard that it was Jesus of Nazareth, he began to shout out and say, "Jesus, Son of David, have mercy on me!" ⁴⁸ Many sternly ordered him to be quiet, but he cried out even more loudly, "Son of David, have mercy on me!" ⁴⁹ Jesus stood still and said, "Call him here." And they called the blind man, saying to him, "Take heart; get up, he is calling you." ⁵⁰ So throwing off his cloak, he sprang up and came to Jesus. ⁵¹ Then Jesus said to him, "What do you want me to do for you?" The blind man said to him, "My teacher, let me see again." ⁵² Jesus said to him, "Go; your faith has made you well." Immediately he regained his sight and followed him on the way.

NKJV

⁴⁶ Now they came to Jericho. As He went out of Jericho with His disciples and a great multitude, blind Bartimaeus, the son of Timaeus, sat by the road begging.⁴⁷ And when he heard that it was Jesus of Nazareth, he began to cry out and say, "Jesus, Son of David, have mercy on me!" ⁴⁸ Then many warned him to be quiet; but he cried out all the more, "Son of David, have mercy on me!" ⁴⁹ So Jesus stood still and commanded him to be called. Then they called the blind man, saying to him, "Be of good cheer. Rise, He is calling you." ⁵⁰ And throwing aside his garment, he rose and came to Jesus. ⁵¹ So Jesus answered and said to him, "What do you want Me to do for you?" The blind man said to Him, "Rabboni, that I may receive my sight." ⁵² Then Jesus said to him, "Go your way; your faith has made you well." And immediately he received his sight and followed Jesus on the road."

DISCOVERY

1. Why was it necessary for Jesus to go to Jerusalem? What did that have to do with his messianic mission?

2. Could Bartimaeus's throwing off his cloak suggests that he envisioned the recovery of his sight?

3. Read 2 Samuel 7:4-17 and Psalm 89:3-4. What connection is Mark attempting to make between King David, Jesus, and Jerusalem? (See also Isa. 11:1f; Jer.23:5f; Ezek. 34:23f.)

4. Why do you think Mark only gave the name of this blind beggar and none of the other individuals healed by Jesus?

5. Is it possible to conclude that Mark recorded these healing stories to reveal to his readers that Jesus is, in fact, the Son of God—the Messiah of Israel?

6. Read Isaiah 29:18; 35:5-6; 53:4-10; 61. How do these scriptures define Jesus' redemptive mission as the Son of God?

ENCOURAGEMENT

Mark set the last healing miracle Jesus performed outside of Jericho. Jericho is located about five miles west of the Jordan and eighteen miles northwest of Jerusalem. The crowd of pilgrims were on their way to the Temple in Jerusalem to attend the Passover feast. Mark alluded that Jesus and his disciples were not just on their way to attend the Passover feast, but that Jesus was on his way to Jerusalem to give his life as a ransom for sin. This is important because Mark's theology of Jesus, the Son of God, is also the suffering servant of God bringing salvation to Israel. All the healing miracles point to God's personal care for his people. The healing miracles are significant signs that the gospel of God's kingdom has drawn near to God's people. Jesus instructed his disciples to proclaim this fact as they healed the sick and called people to repent:

> *"Whatever city you enter, and they receive you, eat such things as are set before you. And heal the sick there, and say to them, 'The kingdom of God has come near to you'" (Luke 10:8-9, NKJV).*

Jesus' kingdom work ushered the kingdom of God into the human realm, offering healing, wholeness, and salvation to the Jews first and, through the Jewish leaders, to point the Gentiles to the resurrected and healing Christ. Mark wanted his readers to see the connection between healing and salvation and to recognize that Jesus Christ is both Israel's Messiah and the redeemer of the world.

RESPONSE

7. Why was the healing of Bartimaeus, which took place outside of Jericho, so crucial to Jesus' overall ministry?

8. Do you know someone who has received his or sight through prayer or medical intervention?

9. How did Bartimaeus's life change after he received his restored vision?

10. Is there some form of blindness in you that Jesus needs to heal?

GOING DEEPER

Think about what it would be like to be physically blind. The last two men healed by Jesus in the gospel of Mark had both lost their eyesight (8:22-26). Mark did not reveal how long these men had been blind or how they became blind. However, both men strongly wanted to regain their sight. Because they had once experienced living in their world as sighted persons, they realized their loss and the limitations of being blind. Their movement and travel opportunities were limited. They lost most of their independence. Their perspective of life's opportunities also had become restricted. They could no longer observe a beautiful sunrise or a sunset. They could not look into the eyes of their loved ones. Their ability to read the Hebrew Scriptures (the Torah or Pentateuch) or any other written resource was a thing of the past. Their lives were filled with limitations and darkness. Bartimaeus had staked out a place on the main road leading to Jerusalem to beg for a living.

As I thought about the limitations of being blind, my thoughts turn to the limitations sighted people may place upon themselves. People who enjoy perfect vision may be blind in other ways. Some sighted people live in darkness, taking the gift of vision for granted. For example, sighted people take God's beautiful earth for granted, choosing not to be good stewards of our water, earth, natural resources, and air. Many animals and plants are endangered or have become extinct because of such abuses.

What good is it for people to have the ability to see when they hate how they look or the way God created them. They don't like the man in the mirror. They don't like themselves because they are either too short or too tall, too fat or too skinny, too dumb or too smart, too rich or too poor. Many of them don't just hate themselves; they also hate those who don't look or talk like them. Sighted people of different ethnic groups have been fighting each other for centuries because of their differences. All of this is an insult to their Creator.

Whether a person is blind or sighted, it all comes down to one's perspective. If our hearts have been cleansed and our minds renewed through the new birth, life takes on new meaning and purpose in Christ Jesus. When a person has been born again, God gives him or her a new life and a new perspective on living. Believers discover that they are to see life and the world through the eyes of Jesus Christ. The New Testament teaches us that believer in Christ, walk by faith and not by sight. Our real sight is through a regenerated heart and renewed mind, which is greater than physical sight.

As we complete this study, meditate on these two passages of scripture in the epistles of John. Consider them as you seek a holistic lifestyle to promote health and wholeness in your life and also encourage the same for your loved ones. John reminds us that this is God's will for you: *"Dear friends, if we don't feel guilty, we can come to God with bold confidence. And we will receive from him whatever we ask because we obey him and do the things that please him"* (I John 3:21- 22, NLT). *"Dear friend, I hope all is well with you and that you are healthy in body as you are strong in spirit"* (3 John 1:2, NLT).

God wants everyone to enjoy wholeness or well-being. Jesus healed the whole person because he understood the body and spirit connection. He could have only healed the paralytic's physical body. However, he healed him spiritually as well as physically. The apostle John also made the connection between the body and spirit. He understood that if our spirit is healthy and whole, we will experience more health in all the other dimensions of life.

DEVOTION

Creator God, thank you for giving me the ability to see and to experience your beautiful creation. Thank you for creating me just the way I am. Not only do I thank you for creating me, but also for how and why you created me. I am fearfully and wonderfully made. My delight is to fulfill my destiny in advancing your kingdom work.

Keep me in good health and empower me to do your kingdom work on earth as it is in heaven. In Jesus' name, amen.

JOURNALING
Give thanks for this study, for the participants, and the facilitators. How has God prepared you through this study to bring healing, wholeness, and salvation to this fractured and sin-infested world? What will be your response?

ABOUT THE AUTHOR

§

Dr. John I. Penn Is a retired ordained United Methodist minister. From 2002 to 2008, Penn served as the pastor of Simpson United Methodist Church in Wilmington, Delaware. Before coming to Simpson, Penn served seven-and-a-half years as the Director of Spiritual Formation and Healing at Upper Room Ministries. As an ordained minister, he has served several pastorates in the Peninsula-Delaware Annual Conference. He has served the church for thirty-five years. Penn has served in two cross-racial appointments as associate pastor.

Dr. Penn is a native of Roanoke, Virginia. He is the author of several books: *Rediscovering Our Spiritual Gifts* (Upper Room Books), a companion workbook for Dr. Charles Bryant's book of the same title; *Getting Well, A Study for Children about Spiritual and Physical Healing* (initially published by Abingdon Press); *Equipped to Serve, A Study for Children about the Gifts of the Holy Spirit*, and *About Caring and Healing, An Activities and Coloring Book for Children.*

He has also written booklets for youth and adults: *What Everyone Should Know about Healing* (Companion to *About Caring and Healing*); *Understanding the Gifts of the Holy Spirit*; and *About the Gifts of the Holy Spirit.*

Dr. Penn holds degrees from the University of Arkansas at Pine Bluff (Bachelor of Science in Music Education), Oral Roberts University (Master of Theology), Eastern Baptist Theological Seminary [now Palmer Theological Seminary] (Master of Divinity), and Wesley Theological Seminary (Doctor of Ministry).

Dr. Penn enjoys playing tennis, writing, gardening, composing music, reading, and listening to jazz. He is married to Gloria J. Parker Penn, the author of *Miracles Still Happen*. They have been blessed with six children (one deceased), ten grandchildren, and three great-grandchildren.

SELECTED BIBLIOGRAPHY

Barclay, William. *The Gospel of Mark*. Philadelphia: The Westminster Press 1975.

Basham, Don. *Deliver Us from Evil*. Grand Rapids: Chosen Books, 1972, 2005.

Hurtado, Larry W. *New International Biblical Commentary*. Massachusetts: *Hendrickson Publisher*, 1983, 1989.

Kelsey, Morton. *Healing and Christianity*. San Francisco: Harper and Row, 1995.

Kingsbury, J. D. *The Christology of Mark's Gospel*. Philadelphia: Fortress, 1983.

Lane, William. L. *The Gospel of Mark: The New International Commentary on the New Testament*. Grand Rapids: Eerdmans, 1974.

MacArthur, John. *The MacArthur Bible Commentary*. Nashville: Thomas Nelson, 2005.

MacNutt, Francis. *Deliverance from Evil Spirits*. Grand Rapids: Chosen Books, 1995, 2009.

Wiersbe, Warren W. *Be Diligent, NT Mark*. Colorado Spring: David C. Cook, 1987.

END NOTES

An Introduction to the Gospel of Mark

1   Barclay, William. *The Gospel of Mark.* Philadelphia: The West-minster Press (1975), 1.
2   Ibid., 2.
3   Ibid., 3.
4   Ibid., 5.
5   Lane, William. L. *The Gospel of Mark: The New International Commentary on the New Testament.* Grand Rapids: Eerdmans (1974), 17.
6   Barclay, 8 and Wiersbe, 18.
7   Barclay, 8.
8   Lane, 601.
9   Barclay, 5.

Healing Moment One: The Healing Power of Jesus' Words

1   Hurtado, Larry W. *New International Biblical Commentary.* Massachusetts: Hendrickson Publisher (1983, 1989), 27.
2   Kingsbury, Jack Dean. *The Christology of Mark's Gospel.* Philadelphia: Fortress Press, (1893), 83-84.
3   Ibid., 83.

4   Lane, William L. *The Gospel of Mark*. The New International Commentary on the New Testament. Grand Rapids: Eerdmans (1974), 74-75.

5   Ibid., 100.

6   MacNutt, Francis. *Deliverance from Evil Spirits,* Grand Rapids: Chosen Books (1995, 2009).

7   Amorth, Gabriele. *An Exorcist Tells His Story.* Ignatius Press, San Francisco, (1999), 33.

8   Martin, Malachi, *Hostage to the Devil: the possession and exorcism of five living Americans.* San Francisco, Harper Collins (1976), 462.

Healing Moment Three: Jesus Identifies with Human Brokenness

1   Lane, William L. *The Gospel of Mark*. The New International Commentary on the New Testament. Grand Rapids: Eerdmans (1974), 85.

Healing Moment Five: Healing is Always Lawful

1   MacArthur, John. *The MacArthur Bible Commentary.* Nashville: Thomas Nelson (2005), 1203.

2   Ibid., 1203.

3   Ibid., 1203.

4   Ibid., 1204.

5   Ibid., 1204.

6   Iverson, Daniel. "Spirit of the Living God."

Healing Moment Seven: Jesus' Power Knows No Bounds

1   Wiersbe, Warren W. *Be Diligent, NT Mark.* Colorado Spring: David C. Cook, (1987), 62.

Healing Moment Nine: Jesus' Supreme Power

1   John 11:23-26, NKJV.

Healing Moment Eleven: Healing Faith, Not Magic

1   Lane, 237-238.

Healing Moment Thirteen: God's Healing Grace Includes Everyone

1   Lane, William L. *The Gospel of Mark*. The New International Commentary on the New Testament. Grand Rapids: Eerdmans (1974), 266.
2   Ibid., 266-267.

Healing Moment Fourteen: A Miracle that Required Two Attempts

1   Pickett, Wilson. "Nine-Nine and One-Half Won't Do."
2   Lane, 285.
3   MacArthur, 1223.
4   Hurtado, 133.

Healing Moment Fifteen: Prayer, Not Human Power, Overcomes Demons

1   Lane, William L. *The Gospel of Mark*. The New International Commentary on the New Testament. Grand Rapids: Eerdmans (1974), 331.
2   Ibid., 335.
3   Ibid., 336.

Healing Moment Sixteen: Your Faith Has Made You Well

1   Lane, 387; Psalm 42:4.

Printed in the United States
by Baker & Taylor Publisher Services